Bridges
Between
Life
and
Death

Dedicated to my beloved grandmother Elena

With heart-warm thanks
to Philip and Thomas on this side,
as well as to Markus and Stefan, Ajra, Albert
and Grigore on the other side

Translated by Cynthia Hindes

First published in German as *Brücken zwischen
Leben und Tod: Begegnungen mit Verstorbenen*
by Verlag Freies Geistesleben, Stuttgart in 2018
First published in English by Floris Books, Edinburgh in 2021
Second printing 2023

 Also available as an eBook

British Library CIP available
ISBN 978–178250–645–4
Printed in Poland through Hussar

Bridges Between Life and Death

Iris Paxino

Floris Books

Contents

Foreword

Modern-day consciousness, bound as it is to the senses, believes that death extinguishes the human being, that there is no afterlife. But the deceased are not dead. What animated their body – their essence, their consciousness, their spirit – lives on in another form in a spiritual world interwoven with our earthly one. The departed have not ceased to exist, nor have we ceased to exist for them. They love and need us just as much as we love and need them.

Iris Paxino knows this from personal experience. By following Rudolf Steiner's anthroposophical path of development, she has cultivated the spiritual capacities, latent in all of us, that allow her to perceive and interact with the so-called dead and the worlds they inhabit after death. Writing from her own experiences with the deceased, she describes the process of dying and the moment of death itself. She gives examples of the unique nature of those who die as children, and the difficulties experienced by those who die by violence or who take their own life. She offers a detailed picture of the afterlife and illuminates the various stages a soul goes through on its journey after death.

Paxino shows that what we take into the spiritual world is what we have cultivated in this life. If we develop an awareness of the truth about the spiritual world, about our guardian angel and the continued existence of those who have predeceased us, then when we cross the threshold at death, we are able to perceive them and work with them. If, however, we have lived a life concerned only with material existence, then in the life after death we struggle to find our bearings.

Our participation in the lives of the departed, and our understanding of their journey through the afterlife, carries great significance for the progress of humankind. Iris Paxino offers a path of practical help based on the possibility of developing a fruitful relationship with the departed. She also describes ways of engaging in redemptive work to help those who experience particular difficulties in the life after death.

In my work as a priest, I have found this book incredibly helpful. I have been able to use Paxino's concrete examples to assure people that their loved ones, along with their guardian angel, will be present and accompany them through their own deaths. I can reassure them that the neighbouring dimension where the so-called dead exist is interwoven with our own, and thus that their loved ones are still present and active. It is comforting to know that it is still possible to create an active connection with their loved ones, and it can help explain some otherwise mysterious phenomena.

Paxino's heartening illustrations are an encouragement to open ourselves up to their inspiration. But most of all her examples help us to realise that our participation in the afterlives of the deceased can be just as important for them as it is for us. Understanding their journey after death allows us to be conscious of how they can continue to work with us, and how they need us. This is important not only for us and for them, but also for the general progress of humankind on earth and for the earth itself. Working on penetrating the mystery of death together with those who have died is an overlooked but important element in our collective way forward.

Rev. Cynthia Hindes, Kimberton, Pennsylvania

Introduction

*The secret of life
And the secret of death
Are locked in two caskets,
Each of which contains the key
To open the other.*

Mahatma Gandhi

'What would you like to do after your studies, young lady?' the psychology professor asked me right after my final oral exam. He was an older gentleman with alert round eyes and a friendly expression. He did not know me from my time as a student, he had been called in as an outside examiner. Now, as he was packing up his bag, we spoke in passing.

'I would like to do a doctorate on near-death experiences,' I replied, without having to think about it.

The professor turned to me, eyes wide with surprise. 'Near-death? Don't you want to do something else? There are entirely different topics for a doctorate! Your exam was excellent. All doors are open to you now, you do know that don't you?'

I tried to explain to him how fascinating near-death experiences are and that from a scientific point of view this phenomenon is a highly interesting field of research. But as I spoke, I saw his concern give way to disappointment and

9

I realised he was not listening to what I was saying. For him, the word 'death' represented an existential threat; it was as if his thinking was paralysed by it.

The professor closed his bag and, shaking his head, turned to me a final time. 'In any case, I wish you all the best and I congratulate you on your exam. I seriously hope that you will reconsider your doctoral thesis. Really, who wants to occupy themselves with death?' With these words he said goodbye, but as he left I called out after him, 'I do!'

I would encounter this reaction towards the theme of death again and again and in all possible variations, be it scepticism, aversion, or fear; sometimes though I would be met with wonder. For me, however, the path ahead was clear: I threw myself into near-death research.

Death entered my life at the age of eighteen, when my grandmother died unexpectedly from a cerebral haemorrhage as a result of a car accident. My world collapsed. My grandmother had been my favourite person since my earliest childhood and her death left a gaping wound in my soul. To no longer be able to see her was inconceivable. I felt alone, with a never-ending pain and with the question: how can I build bridges between life and death?

Shortly after her death, my grandmother began to appear at regular intervals in my dreams. Although the dream images were partly symbolic, I nevertheless had the unshakable conviction that I was meeting her real nature. The realm of the dream was the means by which her soul could reach my consciousness. These transitional experiences were a great gift for me, but after a few months the dream images made it clear that my grandmother would no longer appear on this level. She said goodbye and has not appeared in my dreams since.

Yet what remained for me was this precious realisation: if my grandmother, now deceased, was able to focus her attention and love on me so strongly that she could communicate with my consciousness, then it must be possible for me to align my awareness in such a way that I could reach her. It was clear to me that my everyday consciousness was not yet trained to move back and forth between worlds; the dream level, the realm of the semi-conscious, was the only means available to me at that time of experiencing an encounter with a deceased person. The search for a more concrete way to experience the world of the dead, in a fully intentional and wakeful way, became my new key question.

I began to read everything I could find about death: the history of religion and philosophy, psychology and theology, scientific treatises and so-called specialist literature. I found much of it to be mediocre and disappointing because what was called 'scientific' was in its fundamental tone only the conventional materialistic dogma of our time: the death of the body meant also the extinction of human consciousness. And whilst I also found many exciting and interesting things, these were based only on theories and hypotheses and did not help me develop a wakeful, conscious approach to the world of the deceased.

It wasn't until I discovered Rudolf Steiner's anthroposophy that I came across concrete descriptions of the human being's path of development after death. Finally, here was a contemporary path of knowledge that provided a more comprehensive picture than any I had so far come across. Although complex, Steiner's descriptions were intellectually clear and open to the spiritual. Here was a modern thinker who spoke a deeply spiritual language out of his own experience. Here I found the first tangible answers to my questions.

Parallel to this, I came across descriptions of near-death experiences. Human beings who were clinically dead or close to death reported their experiences in a condition of consciousness free of the body. It was clear that these were only the first moments, the very first steps in the world after death; yet it was at least the beginning of the path I was seeking. From then on, I began to research the phenomenon of near-death experiences. I visited people who had had such experiences and held conversations and interviews with them. I conducted a scientific study and, contrary to my professor's recommendation, wrote my doctoral thesis on the subject. What affected me most as people spoke about their near-death experiences, was how their whole being changed. From a secret inner source, something streamed through them, clear, living, and carried by love; it was something quite noticeable that shone gently from their eyes.

I also began to practise meditation, and over time a new faculty of perception developed in me. Sensations slowly formed into images that could be explained; inner dialogues turned into spiritual encounters that provided answers to my questions. The starting point of such exercises was always to still my inner being, remaining open and completely silent. In this way I learned, step by step, that we can enter the realm of the dead and that the path that leads us there is a path of the heart. Loving solidarity and a sincere interest in the other are what build a bridge within the soul across the threshold. My experiences with the dead increased: intuitive at first, but gradually they became clearer and more conscious. Over many years, my path led me to a sustained engagement with the theme of death.

Later, as a psychologist in a hospital, I also accompanied people as they crossed the threshold of death. At the bedsides of these dying patients, I was allowed to have intense experiences. I noticed that many patients had spiritual experiences during the dying process. Some of them experienced their guardian angel, who lovingly and patiently helped them in the transition between life and death. Others saw deceased family members or friends who now awaited them on the threshold. Attending such people, we can learn to perceive quite precisely the spiritual events around a dying person. The atmosphere in the room is different from that in other patients' rooms. Light and darkness are more intense. The guardian angel's bearing is more serious and possessed of an exceptionally sacred quality. In some cases, the doppelgänger of the dying person is also noticeable, which can be a challenge both for the person dying and for the people around them. I came to understand that tending to the dying could not be limited to organising the patients' last affairs and encouraging their acceptance and release of their earthly life. This work should also include consciously accompanying them across the threshold and preparing them for what is to come afterwards.

During this time in the hospital I was also able to experience some of the patients after their death. Some of them came, now as spiritual figures, to say goodbye or to thank me for our work together. Others had a plea or a request and needed help from the physical world. It became increasingly clear to me that this work does not end at the threshold but inevitably goes beyond it.

After the clinic, my work was focused on my counselling practice. Here it was necessary to attend to people in life crises: those dealing with personal and professional issues; couples with relationship problems; experiences of separation and loss, and those with depression disorders among other things. I had nothing more to do with the dying, but increasingly with the deceased. Some of them appeared as spiritual figures in connection with clients and were part of a complex of problems to be dealt with; others clung permanently to clients and, unnoticed, caused them difficulties. These were souls who could not let go of specific earthly connections after death and had become trapped in an intermediate world close to the earth.

As time went by, I noticed, even outside of my practice, that there are many such trapped souls who cause mental stress, social difficulties, and even severe mental illness among the living. They can burden people, institutions, and social contexts as well as habitats, houses, and landscapes. Here I met many desperate and disoriented figures. Their numbers are staggeringly high, and their need is great. They are a burden for our world and form a legitimate field of therapeutic-social work. These deceased need help. They need clarification about their condition and a conscious connection to the spiritual reality in which they find themselves. Only through such 'redemptive work' can they continue along their path of development in the afterlife.

Nevertheless, in this work, I have also met deceased people who in turn offer their help. These are powerful, selfless souls who have a motivating and inspiring effect, both within the post-mortem realms and in our world. They can be a valuable support for our personal development as well as decisive contributors to the shaping of the earth. To them, I owe illuminating insights and a deeply fulfilling collaboration. In its diversity, the world of the dead is both a task and a support for us. It immediately surrounds and permeates our world. We affect each other in all that we do, and together we form the great wholeness of human existence.

Without an awareness of our coexistence, progress becomes increasingly difficult. In our society, it is not yet commonplace to recognise our interaction with the dead as a component of our social context. However, with great joy, I increasingly encounter those who are developing a wakeful interest and who are actively contributing to redemptive work. 'We' are therefore no longer just a few. That is why I look with trust into a future in which friendship and connection with the dead will become a reality for more and more people.

When I look at my personal path of development in working with the deceased, the course of an exciting, instructive and wonderful journey unfolds before me. Along the way I have experienced impressive mental and spiritual landscapes, I have had unexpected encounters with many deceased people and made new spiritual friendships. I have come to understand that only a small step of consciousness separates us from the world of the dead. I hope that more people will have the courage to take this step so that a lively and ever more conscious exchange between this world and the hereafter becomes possible. The responsibility for the creation of our shared world can truly allow us to build bridges between life and death. From my heart, I thank all whom I have met along this path, both on this side and on the other side of human existence and from whom I have been allowed to learn so many valuable things! It is in an intimate bond of destiny and with deep gratitude that I dedicate this book to my beloved grandmother, who made possible my very first glimpses across the threshold.

1

Death in the Course of History

There are more things in heaven and earth, Horatio,
Than are dreamt of in your philosophy...

William Shakespeare, *Hamlet*, Act 1, Scene 5

Life and death are the great polarities of human existence on earth. The question of what they mean has accompanied us throughout all human cultures and epochs. Life and death are a part of us; they arise out of one another. Religion, history, philosophy, art, literature and science have always revolved around these greatest mysteries. New answers replace old questions; further questions arise from answers already found. Can life and death be understood as 'being' and 'non-being'? What is the dimension of eternity towards which humanity has always striven? What happens to human beings when they leave this life? Has death always been a mystery to the people of past cultures?

Historical sources tell us that in different ages and cultures there have been different ideas about the fate of human beings after death. What we call the face of death presented itself differently than it does today. Our understanding of death has undergone many transformations over time. All the documents that have been preserved for us testify to the fact that the people of the past did not ask what *death* is, but about what happens to the soul *after* death.

Human beings in the ancient Indian culture felt themselves embedded in a spiritual reality that surrounded them. They felt a longing for this spiritual world, out of which they had been born into earthly existence and which they recognised as true reality. For them, life on earth was an illusion, the great maya. The gate to the hereafter was not closed to them. Death liberated them from the earthly world and the body-bound soul was thus redeemed. Over extended periods of time, this ancient knowledge was handed down in oral form through songs and rhythmic-poetic verses. Later, it flowed into Vedic philosophy, Samkhya and the original yogic streams.

Another formative human epoch, the Sumerian-Babylonian epoch, left us with the moving epic of *Gilgamesh* as an expression of its attitude towards death. This is humanity's first written literary work, and at the same time, the first song of lament for the dead that has been handed down to us. From the twenty-fifth century BC onwards it was passed down orally, and in the eighteenth century BC it was written down in cuneiform script. It bears witness to the fact that Gilgamesh experienced the death of his close friend Enkidu as a terrible loss and set off to bring him back. Here death is a drastic, painful separation, but it is not an impassable border. It is not a mystery; rather, it is a challenge for human beings.

Another advanced civilisation that left us with evidence of their way of life is the Egyptian epoch. *The Egyptian Book of the Dead*, the myth of Isis and Osiris, and the discoveries made in the tombs of the pyramids, speak a language that knew death and placed its roots in the midst of life. The cult of mummification not only meant preserving the corpse but was understood to be a bridge between the physical body and the soul rising into the spiritual world. Death was not the end of life. It was experienced as a sublime gateway to a path of development beyond. Only in the decadent late phase of Egyptian culture did the understanding of the human being's essence shift increasingly into this world. With the downfall of this high civilisation, the cult of mummification degenerated into an attempt to capture and preserve the earthly.

The next great epoch of human development was ancient Greece. This epoch left us with extremely valuable works in the fields of philosophy, poetry, sculpture and architecture. This culture was so rich in content that a variety of intellectual currents could develop in its womb. Homer painted the image of Greek human beings in the context of their world in his masterpieces *The Iliad* and *The Odyssey*. The realm of death was Hades' world: a shadow world in which the souls of the dead lived alone in a disembodied, misty form as an image of their formerly physical body. The Greek feared this underworld. Only the 'heroes', that is, those gifted with special abilities, those trained and filled with courage and carried by love and pain, could penetrate this world and then leave it again as a living human being.

For people of that time, Heraclitus indicated the interconnection of life and death in a clear picture: everything that lives has death in it through the continuous stream of becoming. Death, in turn, always has life in it. Both life and death weave in human life and death. Only in this way can continuous development flow through everything.

But another philosophical approach also emerged in Greek antiquity through Democritus, the father of the Greek atomists.

According to his view, all matter in the world was composed of indivisible particles, or atoms, and it was the movement of these material particles that gave rise to natural processes. Nature was not ensouled. Human beings no longer felt themselves to be part of the divine, which flowed through both nature and human beings. For the first time in the history of humankind, the question arose as to whether the soul – which according to this view also consisted of atoms – goes the way of dissolution when the physical body dies. Death, which until then had accompanied humanity throughout all cultures as part of life, now and only now became a riddle! The germ of the materialistic world view was born through this cultural stream. Although the philosophy of great thinkers like Heraclitus, Plutarch, Socrates, Plato, Aristotle, and many others represents the ferment of the entire further spiritual development of Europe, Democritus' philosophical idea maintained itself, even if only imperceptibly. The soil of the Enlightenment was then fertile for this germ, for from then on atomism was able to unfold into the mighty structure of materialism.

The new Christian culture brought with it a different understanding of death. Although people no longer had the feeling that they could penetrate the realm of the dead during their lifetime, the dead were given a place amid everyday life. Cemeteries were built next to churches in the heart of villages and towns. Death was accepted as a part of life. People often felt its approach. With the family present, a priest often accompanied the process of dying. The dying person blessed their relatives and solemnly bade them farewell.

Increasingly, however, over the course of centuries, human beings lost the connection to death and began to experience it as a threat to life. They struggled with the figure of death, depicted in religious art as the fearsome skeletal figure of the Grim Reaper.

By the beginning of the twentieth century, this tendency had intensified to such an extent that western societies increasingly excluded death from life. The process of dying was transferred to hospitals. Medical staff and relatives often concealed the dying person's critical condition. As far as their feelings were concerned, the dying person was now left to their own devices. Through the many victims of the two World Wars the image arose of the fallen and lonely dying soldier. Here is a new symbol for death, the symbol of the person who dies alone, who disappears far from family and their native soil, often without a name. The anonymity of their life became the anonymity of their death. Consequently, death was 'de-subjectified' and felt to be 'inhumanly cruel' and impersonal. Death no longer belonged to life; it became merely the termination of life. The original connection between life and death was sundered and they became irreconcilable opposites.

A culture has thus emerged which finds the belief in a human soul that exists independently of the body after death wholly irrational. Instead, the idea that the brain produces human consciousness and that consciousness is extinguished at death now dominates all areas of life. Death is declared to be the final extinction of a human being's existence.

The practical and intellectual implications of modern natural sciences and the humanities are so far-reaching that this new world view claims a kind of totalitarian universality. Political systems, as well as schools and universities, are built on its foundation. The view that death is a natural part of life is no longer discussed and thus fear of death grows. Death is taboo.

But this view, although it still permeates our western culture, has already passed its zenith. In the second half of the twentieth century, phenomena such as out-of-body experiences, contact with the afterlife, and memories from before birth were already multiplying. Increasing numbers of people are describing memorable encounters with angels and with Christ, experiences with elemental beings and with the dead. Experiences gained through meditation, suggestive of actual spiritual experiences, continue to accumulate. Ironically, as a result of medical science, a new phenomenon concerning death appears, one that once again questions the modern understanding of the world: the phenomena of near-death experiences. With the help of emergency medical measures, people on the brink of death are brought back to life. These individuals have experienced themselves outside of their body with a clear and awakened consciousness, even though they had been declared clinically dead by medical staff.

Furthermore, they speak of insights into another reality in which they have had encounters with the deceased and spiritual beings. The appalled attempts of science to classify these experiences as organic brain processes, as anxiety-induced or as psychopathological defence reactions, fail. Thousands and thousands of mentally healthy people testify to having had such experiences. Moreover, these experiences confirm each other because whilst the essence and content of each experience may possess an individual quality, they nevertheless follow a common pattern. A change in thinking is taking place. Society is beginning to respond. New medical and psychosocial disciplines are emerging, along with new forms of institutions. The process of dying is receiving renewed attention and appreciation, and in just a few decades a worldwide hospice movement has appeared. Care of the dying and palliative medicine have found their way into clinics and hospitals and have quickly become recognised disciplines. Not only are the physical needs of the patient considered, but also the patient's psychological, social, and spiritual needs.

Accordingly, we find ourselves amid an ideological upheaval and can see with our own eyes how the period of materialistic thinking is already being replaced. Like every historical and spiritual era before it, this cultural epoch has developed specific systems of thought, content, and social forms. But human consciousness is continuously changing and this enables new experiences of reality. The time that has already begun carries with it a new understanding of the dimensions of life and death. It brings new abilities for experiencing spiritual reality and therefore creates a new relationship to the wholeness of human existence, to ourselves as physical, emotional, and spiritual beings who develop through different states of consciousness. Recent controversies over the belief or non-belief in a life after death are now increasingly being replaced by a spirituality based on personal experience. Greater numbers of people are exploring dimensions of consciousness that surpass our daily awareness, dimensions which open insights into an extremely multi-layered, miraculously complex composition of supersensible levels.

The realm of the dead is merely one sequence in this comprehensive structure of meaning. For many, the question of whether there is an existence after death already seems to have been answered: yes! Now it is a question of finding out *how* things continue after the threshold has been crossed. This book sets out to explore the worlds after death step by step.

2

The Process of Dying

In one of the stars I shall be living.
In one of them I shall be laughing,
And so it will be as if all the stars were laughing
When you look at the sky at night . . .
And when your sorrow is comforted . . .
You will be content that you have known me.

Antoine de Saint-Exupéry, *The Little Prince*

Thanatopsychology, the psychology of death, divides the process of dying into three stages: dying, death and thereafter. This correctly points to the fact that death is a dynamic event, which implies a progressive course. From this it is clear that death can be experienced not only at the moment of physical death, but also, in many ways, in advance.

The experiences that take place in the entire phase before death are experiences of dying. First of all, they refer to states that have to do with the body's decline and the person's psychological grappling with death in this last phase of earthly life. This phase is where the classic psychological accompaniment of dying comes in. Regulating unresolved matters and saying goodbye to family and friends is directly involved in this work. Most dying people also feel the need to settle their wills and estates. Some want to clarify their funeral; others are afraid to tackle this topic. These matters form the outer framework and thus the first level of this work.

A second level in accompanying dying people is reviewing their life story. If their condition allows it, creating an overview of their earthly biography is an essential process. Such an overview rounds off their life and generates understanding. This biographical overview enables them to clarify their relationship to themselves, to recognise the great arc of their life and to prepare to accept the transition across the threshold.

With some people, spiritual experiences arise during this work of clarification and detachment, experiences that mark their approaching death through the presence of angels and those already deceased. These experiences form the third and most intimate level of a person's dying process. They show that death is prepared spiritually and announces itself supersensibly.

I remember a sixty-seven-year-old patient in the hospital who had had an extremely challenging illness. Her nature was loving and mild. She had accepted the help of the care-givers modestly and very gratefully. One day I entered her room and the first thing she said was: 'I am expected, you know? I am expected,' and a smile brightened her grey face. The illness had marked her body, her breathing was laboured, and from day to day the pain became more unbearable. 'Yes, I am expected,' she repeated. Her eyes were shining and a joyful glow emanated from her being.

'Would you like to tell me about it?' I asked.

'It's my angel. I know it is him. He is so loving; he waits patiently. He stands mostly at the head end, do you see? Here...' she said, pointing to the wall behind her bed. 'He is so loving

. . . And sometimes I see him in the right corner of the room, there by the window, next to the curtain, you see? But that's rare. Most of the time I feel him back here, with me. Some days other figures appear in the room. My mother is there below. Oh, it was so long ago that she died . . .' The patient's gaze turned inwards and childhood memories from a time long past came to life in her. She told of her mother, of the years they spent together, of her mother's death. 'And you know, she is so young now, much younger than she was then, and so beautiful, so radiant! It is time for me to go. I am expected there. I am no longer afraid; it is only a transition. I know that now.'

A few days later she died in the presence of her partner, calm, collected and with clear consciousness.

A change of scene, another patient's room: a lady, in her mid-fifties, still struggling with her illness. It was hard for her to accept that her life should end so early. One day she whispered to me unexpectedly:

'I keep seeing a figure at the window. I have never believed in anything like this, but she is always there. I am sick, but not crazy. Can you see her too?'

I looked and saw her angel. 'Yes, someone is there. Can you recognise who that is?'

'She seems so familiar to me, the figure, as if I had always known her. But I have never seen her before.' She fell silent for a long time as she contemplated the figure, then the patient's face brightened. Quietly she said: 'It is my Angeline. We usually speak of angels, but for me, she seems like an Angeline.'

It was a special, intimate moment. Her use of the word 'Angeline' was surprising, so it was even more important to allow her to perceive and to describe the experience for herself. From this moment on, the patient's mental state changed. It was like breathing a sigh of relief; she began to accept her illness and we were able to have intense conversations right up until her death.

Another patient, a rather rough and not very friendly older woman, who had been bedridden for quite some time, received me one day. She was in her bed as usual but dressed as if ready to go out. She had put on her jewellery and her beautifully knitted woollen jacket. Her shoes stood next to each other by the bed. 'What's going on?' I asked. 'Where do you want to go?'

'I'm being picked up,' she replied. 'My mother came.' My mind began calculating the patient was in her early eighties, meaning her mother must be at least a hundred years old, so she could not have meant that. It became clear to me what this was about, but I did not want to pre-empt her.

'What do you mean? Is your mother still alive?' I asked.

'No, of course not,' she replied, 'but she came anyway. This morning, there.' She pointed to the corner of the room. 'She stood there. I saw her very clearly.'

'Oh? And what did your mother say?'

'She said, "I will come and get you. We are already waiting for you." She was so beautiful and young, my mother. She looked as young as when I was a child, and she was all made of light.'

After a pause, the patient added in her own blunt way, 'So that means I am going now. I have to go now, don't I?'

I looked at the lady again more closely. Despite her advanced age and her very serious illness, she did not give the impression of being directly at the threshold. Until the meeting mentioned above, she had not been able to look back on her life or to shape her dying process in any way. Quite harsh to all who surrounded her, she had until then refused more in-depth conversations. However, through the encounter with her deceased mother, her defiant attitude had given way to clarity and openness. I then told her: 'We all have to leave at some point, and of course you will, too. But I don't have the impression that you have to leave right now. It is very nice that your mother was here, and it is wonderful to know you are expected. But now let's see if you still have something to do here. Is there anything else you want to do? Are you really ready to say goodbye to this life?'

Now conversation was finally possible. Touched by the appearance of her mother's spirit, the patient opened up about her childhood and her later life. We talked about her experiences, the blows of destiny that had been shaped by war, as well as more beautiful and joyful moments from her life. Because she was suffering from dementia we could not work through her life in any kind of a structured way, but individual pictures and colourful moods lit up again in her soul. After only a few weeks she died peacefully. In keeping with her nature, she chose a moment when she was all alone.

Working with dying people has made clear to me the importance of biographical work, even if it only comes at the very end of life. The fact that there is someone who carefully asks questions, who listens attentively, creates a sensitive, pure space of perception. The more trusting and open the patient is, the more receptive they become to the inner truth of their earthly life. Events appear to them in a new light, connections and rhythms can be revealed, and repressed moments can, at least partially, be brought to light. Even painful things can be healed emotionally. The person facing the threshold has the opportunity to clarify and resolve many things, which will have a positive effect on their death process as well as on their later post-death development.

Unresolved and repressed experiences have a strongly inhibiting effect after death. Therefore, if such things are recognised, named, and accepted as belonging to our self even before we cross the threshold, it has a liberating effect.

Forgiveness is decisive in this process: forgiveness of others and – no less important – of oneself. In many lives we encounter difficult relationships, guilt, resentment, unmastered anger and unresolved strife. If the situation makes it possible, it is helpful if the dying person clarifies and resolves these matters personally with others. But if mutual discussions are no longer possible, even a purification process carried out alone is helpful and healing. Doing so creates a spiritual connection and that affects the ensuing relationship.

It also happens that at the end of their lives people want to clarify something with someone who has already died. In these cases they always express regret that they can no longer reach the person, for example, to ask for forgiveness. But here, too, the dying person can be encouraged to turn inwardly to the deceased and to express what is in their heart. This also has a very real effect and is much more directly absorbed by the dead than is generally imagined.

Consciously working with our biography brings clarity and purification. It creates a deep gratitude for the past and for the miracles and gifts of our unique biography. The course of each life has its own signature, its riches and its pains, which in turn contribute to a person's development and fulfil a deep meaning. In looking at the biographical arc of a life, the power of the higher self that created this incarnation and was the guide in the decisive events of this life shines forth.

It is also possible to take a close look at the impulses that a person could not implement in this lifetime. What omissions were there? Which opportunities were not used? It is by no means a question of evaluating these things as personal failures, but of taking them with us as germs for a further future. The human life that is ending not only draws a reflexive arc over the past that has already been lived, it also sketches a curve of destiny into the future. Our angel guards these processes of knowledge and reveals them to the deceased again during their time in the soul world after death. The more consciously we take with us everything that belongs to us as an impulse for further development, the more vigilantly and concretely we can take up and develop these themes and motifs in a future incarnation.

It would be desirable if such aspects of biographical work, which round off the arc of a life lived, were more actively incorporated into the care of dying persons. Likewise, it is important to take seriously the spiritual perceptions and experiences that occur during the dying process and to include them in the biography. We can become a worthy conversational partner for the dying by refining and training our perceptive capacities.

One day I entered the room of a woman with cancer. She was in her late forties, the mother of four children. For weeks her entire family had been worried about whether the treatment would work. When I went into her room that day, there was a deep, holy seriousness. I paused for a moment and tried to sense what was there. There seemed to be many figures present. At the patient's head stood her angel, with arms spread out around her in an enveloping gesture. It was as if he were carrying her, even though she was lying in bed. The angel's head bent over her, his expression dignified, compassionate and waiting. At the side of the bed stood the patient's deceased parents-in-law, gently smiling and also silently waiting. Then it became clear to me that her death, which happened a few weeks later, had already been decided on the spiritual level.

The presence of spiritual beings is not a sign that a person is on the threshold, for they are also present during illness and other life situations. The threshold, however, has its own unique characteristics, which can be seen and accompanied consciously.

In former times sick and dying people were cared for in the circle of their family. They could say goodbye to this life at home, respected in their familiar environment. Nowadays in our society, most people die in hospitals or old people's homes. This makes it even more important to create spaces of awareness for them and to generate a protective, healing atmosphere so that they can experience this transition in dignity and peace.

3

The Moment
of Death

The body will tear like a garment, but I, the well-known I, I am.

Johann Wolfgang von Goethe,
Wilhelm Meister's Apprenticeship

Anyone who has been present at a person's death knows how inexpressibly moving this event is. During a natural dying process, there is usually a peaceful, luminous crossing of the threshold of death, in which we can witness a truly sacred moment. The soul's transition from the physical to the spiritual world has the appearance of a resurrection.

At the moment of death, a person's higher spiritual members free themselves from the physical body. These include the life body, which maintains life in the physical body and is also the seat of memory, the soul body, which bears the person's consciousness and which is permeated by the highest member, the person's 'I'. With spiritual sight, we can see how the spirit figure of the dying person detaches itself from the body and floats above it. This usually happens via the head, but can also occur via the heart in some instances. Whereas the soul detaches itself quickly from the physical body, the life body does so more slowly and can still be felt surrounding the physical body for a period of time. On average this lasts for around three days, but there can be considerable deviations in the length of time. In animals, for example in a mouse or a small bird, the pulsing release of the life body takes only a few minutes. For domestic animals that had a strong connection to their human environment, this can take between one and several hours.

At the moment of their death, the spiritual figure of the deceased human being is still clearly recognisable as a human figure. It floats above the lifeless physical body, and is surrounded by light. At the same time, it shines out of itself in a certain way. Since the life body is the bearer of memory, the entire tableau of the life just lived unfolds before the deceased human being, which they now experience as a comprehensive life review. Usually, all experiences here occur at the same time. The deceased views their life as though looking out from a mountain top over a broad landscape. Next to and surrounding the spirit figure of the deceased there are always several angelic beings present. Symbolically speaking, the guardian angel, who usually stood behind the human being during their incarnation, now steps forward and becomes 'visible' to them. Other angelic beings join the angel, surrounding the one who has crossed the threshold. For all these angelic beings the eternal self or 'I' of this human being and the entire sequence of their incarnations are clearly perceptible, from the very beginning and through all their stages.

Furthermore, figures of deceased people, who during the time of incarnation were connected with the one who has just died, appear at the transition into the spiritual world. Usually, they are close relatives, friends or companions who have already crossed the threshold. With loving gentleness and heartfelt joy they receive the newcomer, helping to form a bridge between worlds.

The elemental beings in the room also react very strongly to a human being's moment of death. They gather around the scene like fascinated children eager to learn. For them, too, the shining 'I' of the deceased reveals itself, albeit in a form different from that perceived by the angels. They see the significance of this human being for the evolution of the earth and what they have inscribed on the earth through their incarnations.

The moment of death is therefore never a moment of loneliness. The hierarchies receive the deceased person in a sublime ceremony, as that which goes dark in the world of the bereaved shines forth on the other side in a luminous spiritual celebration. For the one crossing the threshold it is as though they 'breathe' themselves out of the physical world. It is a moment of liberation and they experience an incredible expansion of their being. They look down at their body and realise it is merely a shell they have discarded. Their consciousness in the spiritual world is clear and wide awake; they recognise the beings that now receive them. For the deceased it is a sacred moment in which their individuality, embedded in the light of an elevated spiritual reality, unfolds within them more intensely than before.

It is not necessary to be physically present to perceive a person crossing the threshold. For example, there are reports from the time of the World Wars that describe how at the moment of a soldier's death he appeared to his mother or wife at home. Subsequently it was found that the time of the appearance coincided with the soldier's time of death in battle. In our time too, people have reported that they perceived from a distance the death of a close friend or relative, who appeared to them as a figure of light. A deep, heartfelt love helps to create the connection between the deceased and the bereaved.

At the beginning of my hospital work, I had a moving encounter with an eighty-nine-year-old lady. During my first visit with the doctors, the patient's dressings had to be changed. The wounds were deep. The patient tried to suppress a moan, but with every touch, she flinched in torment. Her face was distorted with pain; her wide-open eyes looked at me. I bent over to her, held her hand, and we looked at each other in silence. In the afternoon I returned to her room, this time alone. The lady slept, exhausted from the arduous procedure that morning. I sat down quietly on a chair and looked at her. Her body was emaciated. Her bones pushed through the blanket. Her painfully curved figure looked like that of a small, scrawny girl. I wondered what destiny this woman had had to bear in her long life, and I began to say a prayer for her in silence. In the evening, I came back to speak to her relatives. The patient noticed me immediately, her little dark eyes sparkled, and she said:

'Ah, you were here earlier today!'

'Yes,' I said, 'during the morning rounds.'

'No, no, you were here in the afternoon when I was asleep.'

'But you were fast asleep. How did you know?'

She smiled. 'Oh, child, when you're between the worlds you look at both sides. Where I am now, the doors open again and again, here and over there.' She then moved a little closer and added: 'The Lord's Prayer was beautiful as you spoke it.'

I said I was surprised by this, as I had not spoken the prayer aloud.

'Do you think it makes a difference?' she said and smiled again. 'Thoughts and everything within are a reality on the other side. Yes, it's a threshold.'

Many more intense conversations followed in the coming days. Biographical memories were mixed with spiritual perceptions that the patient had during this final time in hospital. The apparent confusion of her stories, which sometimes overwhelmed her family members, were by no means a confused, disjointed tangle of thoughts. When I turned my inner attention towards her, I could feel when she was moving between levels of consciousness. I accompanied her on wonderful journeys through her long, eventful life. In her youth she had been fluent in five languages, and now they emerged, alternating with each other and colouring the various events of her life. She delighted in switching from French to English, in singing Italian songs and reciting Russian poems, before effortlessly quoting Goethe's *Faust* in German. And then, after these escapades, she would fall asleep, exhausted, the room still full of her laughter and mischievous joy. Given how frail she was, I often wondered where she got all this energy from.

At other times, however, her mood changed. She left the realm of earthly memories and made you aware of another reality that surrounded her.

'Sometimes it gets so bright in the room. It fills with a bright and beautiful light, and there is such a loving power in it. Everything is light, everything is love, everything is one, and we are part of it, we are embedded in it.'

Another time she said: 'There is a figure who sits in the corner of the room and waits. She is mostly there when I am alone, but also sometimes when you are here. Can you see her? There, in the corner of the room.'

'Can you describe this figure to me?' I asked.

'Yes, she is bright and beautiful and made of light. I can also see her when I close my eyes. She looks like a woman, although she is not a woman. We only say that because she is as beautiful as a woman and for us a woman is the most beautiful thing we know. But she is much, much more beautiful, and made entirely of light.'

'Who is this figure?'

'I don't know. I think it is my angel, but I don't know exactly. I will know when I am over there.'

During these days the patient shared further impressive experiences of this kind. When I had a few days off, and we both knew that her time was near, she asked me to speak the Lord's Prayer once again, this time with her. I held her small, bony hand, and as we looked intensely into each other's eyes we spoke the prayer, word by word, line by line. It was a deeply moving experience and I left with tears in my eyes, grateful to have encountered this extraordinary woman.

Two nights later, I woke around 4.00 am. It was a cold, quiet winter's night; the moon cast its light into the room. Suddenly I was aware of a figure just above me and recognised the spirit of this dear patient. A gentle, luminous atmosphere emanated from her. She said that her time had come and that she felt completely free and full of peace. She wanted to say goodbye and to thank me again for the time we had shared. She said we would meet again, and that I must not forget that she would always be close by. I felt once more all the warmth of her soul, and then her figure dissolved. I looked back at the clock: it was 4.07 am.

After dawn, I dressed and drove to the clinic. The nurses on the ward were surprised to see me.

'Doctor, what are you doing here? You are not on duty today, are you?'

'Mrs B. died tonight, didn't she? Do you know what time that was?'

'Yes, she died shortly after 4.00 am. But how do you know that?'

'Just a feeling,' I replied.

I entered the patient's room where the lady had been washed and cleaned by the nurses. They had dressed her in a beautiful white dress. Despite her countless wrinkles, she looked almost like a young girl. Flowers had been strewn across her bed. It was a beautiful sight. There was a loving smile on her face and her expression remained gently radiant until the funeral, just as I had experienced her on the night of her death. She was my first patient to die. To this day I am deeply grateful to her for letting me share her death in this way.

Rarely have I experienced such a harmonious dying and death process. Despite the pain of her illness, this woman had accepted and affirmed her fate. She was present in every moment and her soul was as joyful and as open as that of a child. All of this had lent a dignified beauty to the moment of death. If a person's death can happen in this way, then it is indeed a gift of grace.

But it is not always the case that a person dies in this way. Their physical state, their mental condition, their conscious and unconscious attitude towards death, as well as the nature of their death, play a decisive role. Just like their birth, a person's death has its own individual signature.

4

Difficulties Crossing
the Threshold

Friend, as you are, do not remain so;
From one light forth to another go.

Angelus Silesius, *The Cherubinic Wanderer*

The impact of our culture on how we view death creates an immediate sense of anxiety that varies in quality and intensity from person to person. There are different forms of fear, conscious or unconscious, overwhelming or creeping, overt or subtle. But in all its forms, fear binds the soul's experience and restricts its perception. A defensive attitude towards death is reflected in the process of dying. This anxiety can lead so far that the dying process resembles more a battle than a release. Fear also has a direct effect on our experience in the afterlife. If the soul's light is darkened, then its ability to perceive in its new environment is severely limited.

Our personal relationship with the spiritual dimensions of being also plays a decisive role in our crossing the threshold. Having a religious or a spiritual background, however, is no guarantee of a liberated death. I was astonished when I realised that many people's faith is somewhat theoretical in nature. In the face of death, they experience doubt, despair, insecurity and fear; a sincere 'trust in God' is not truly anchored in their nature. Lifelong churchgoers and people of all spiritual persuasions are not exempt from this. The theoretical conceptions that we formed in life are not decisive here. We could say that what has been truly felt and lived – the 'spirituality of our own soul' – is the power that ignites our light of consciousness in the spiritual world.

There are also *types* of deaths that cause difficulty crossing the threshold. These are situations in which death occurs unexpectedly or violently. Accidents, disasters, war, murder, or suicide can cause a massive shock to the individual concerned. Here death occurs in a brutal way, emotionally as well as physically. The soul is literally torn from the body and usually experiences fear, horror, helplessness and despair. The trauma can be so great that these people do not understand what has happened to them. They are deeply shaken and feel confused and disoriented. In such cases it is even more important to have a calming and enlightening effect. Often, a prayer spoken inwardly helps as a first step. The Lord's Prayer is one of the most effective prayers. It is the most widespread in our culture and reaches nearly every soul. Such a prayer helps those who have crossed the threshold to revive their inner light and to become aware of the spiritual reality that now surrounds them.

It is not necessarily the case that a sudden death so confuses the deceased that they do not understand what is happening. Some experience themselves floating above the event. They look at their lifeless body from above and immediately feel detached from it. They perceive that they have entered another dimension of being and orient themselves quickly in it. But prayer is still a valuable help in these cases. It gives warmth of soul and inner peace and makes it easier for those who have died to cross the threshold.

I once drove past a very bad road accident. Several cars were wedged into each other, one more was overturned and another was further away on the embankment. Police, fire brigade, an emergency doctor and several ambulances were already in attendance. The scene of the accident had been cordoned off and I could see police officers coordinating what was going on. Other people stood in small groups around the vehicles. Then I passed the accident site. At the next opportunity, I stopped and got out of my car. I concentrated on the scene of the accident to see whether any seriously injured or deceased person needed help. I saw the figure of a young man floating a few metres above the scene. He looked at the events from above and did not seem to fully understand what had happened. Suddenly I saw a warm beam shining towards him from below. This ray came from an older woman who stood next to the accident on the side of the road, quietly reciting the Lord's Prayer. She had not seen the spiritual form of the young man, only his body as it lay covered on the roadside. Filled with compassion, she said this prayer for the unknown dead man who perceived it as a gleaming ray of warmth. It pacified his soul and he was able to take his eyes off the scene of the accident. As soon as he did, he saw several angelic beings gathered around him and after a few moments he left with them.

It is by no means a requirement that we must be able to 'see' the deceased person in order to help them. Just the knowledge of such connections and direct action is enough to make a difference.

But it is not only sudden or unexpected death that can be confusing for the person concerned. A diminished or weakened state of consciousness at the time of death, for example as a result of the effects of pain-relieving medicines, can lead to the deceased person only dimly perceiving their crossing of the threshold. If the soul's awareness or perception of pain is artificially restricted, then the transition into the spiritual world is likewise undergone in a reduced state of consciousness. This can give rise to astonishment and incomprehension in the excarnating human being.

One night our then four-year-old son screamed and said he was very cold. It was a warm June night, but I noticed that the atmosphere in the apartment was unusually chilly. I covered up our son and went back into the bedroom, where I was met by the radiant spirit figure of a woman. I stopped in amazement and tried to sense who it was. I eventually recognised in her a dear friend. She had had a long and severe illness. She had always refused to take painkillers, but in the last stage this had been unavoidable. That night she had crossed the threshold and now here she was in our apartment. She seemed calm and peaceful, and she was shrouded in a quiet, moon-like white light. The figure of her life body seemed small and extremely thin, giving the impression of profound exhaustion. She looked like someone who had just 'breathed herself out'. She was amazed at her own condition and at the possibility of unexpectedly being able to go through the night to people she knew. She seemed to be in a kind of dream state, not consciously awake. She did not speak to me, nor did she react to my words, but it was nevertheless an exceptionally beautiful encounter. She looked around for a while and seemed to want to understand what was happening. Then she disappeared from our apartment like a gentle breeze. The next day I was told that she had died that night.

Here, the moment of death did not take place with the same clear, sun-like awareness that would have been the case had medication not been prescribed. The consciousness of this dying friend was subdued. She realised she had crossed the threshold, but it seemed like a dream to her at first and hence her transition had a more moon-like quality to it.

Such cases are not serious because with time the consciousness of the deceased clears and they can then perceive the spiritual world that now surrounds them. However, there are severe cases in which the deceased does not realise they have died. This can happen through strong consciousness-dampening medications as well as drugs. The affected people are in a dulled state of consciousness and at the moment of death they do not even notice the transition into the spiritual world. They 'sleep through' their demise. This lowered consciousness can also occur in people who have been seriously ill or bedridden for a long time in a somnolent state and have lost their connection to space and time. Some of them persist in this vegetative state and do not even register that they have left their bodies. For example, we frequently find such deceased persons in old people's homes and nursing homes. They are perceptible in their former rooms and can remain in this intermediate state for months or even years.

In situations like these, it is important that immediately after death the relatives and survivors tell the deceased that they have left the physical world. This can take place in a calm and clear inner dialogue: 'You have now died. You can let go of your body and feel free, without pain and physical limitation. Look around you, and you will perceive other spiritual forms.'

We can always help if we have the impression that the person crossing the threshold is disoriented, confused or insecure. It is crucial to make them aware that they are no longer in the earthly world and that they must reorient themselves in their new spiritual environment. We can direct their attention to spiritual occurrences and make them understand that they can receive help and orientation through their guardian angel or those deceased relatives and friends who are receiving them. The decisive factor here is that those concerned now experience their *own* motivation to detach from the earth and to turn towards the spiritual world.

The moment of death is therefore always individual and shaped by the person's awareness and experience. The quality of their consciousness determines how they perceive their entry into the spiritual world and which spiritual beings they recognise. A luminous, clear, trusting transition across the threshold enables them to identify their spiritual homeland and to re-encounter their closest friends, their guardian angel, and close deceased relatives. On the other hand, an unconscious, frightened or darkened state of mind can make it much more difficult to perceive these beings of light. Dark or demonic beings can be experienced here, since they too are part of our soul experience. All of this shapes our experience of the moment of death.

Objectively, however, and without exception, at the moment of death every person is taken up and received lovingly by the spiritual beings closest to them.

The spiritual world always welcomes home its returning travellers.

5

In the Time
After Death

Cast care aside, give over grieving:
Nothing is here for fear.
Think but of one casting a bell, believing
Its first pure note to hear
When once the mold is broken.
Your mold, too, is a token
Of that which death will tell
When once the sweeping hammer blow sets ringing
The liberated bell.
So from its mold your soul soars singing.

Manfred Kyber, *Genius Astri*

During the first days after physical death, the excarnated person lives on in their etheric or life body and can be perceived relatively easily in the spiritual world.

According to Rudolf Steiner, all living things possess an etheric or life body. This is the life-filled spirit-form that permeates every part of the physical body, binding its substances together and filling it with life. The etheric body remains bound to the physical body throughout a person's lifetime and departs from it only at death. The physical body then begins to decay, its substances returning to the earth, whilst the etheric body continues on into the spiritual world together with the other higher members of the human being.

In appearance the deceased still resembles their former physical form. They also show themselves to the inner eye as though they were wearing the appropriate earthly clothes. These characteristics are a clear indication of their existence in that part of the spiritual world closest to the earth, the etheric world. As soon as the deceased enters higher spheres, their spiritual appearance changes for our perception.

The etheric body is the bearer of our memories, thoughts, habits and life processes. When it is released from its attachment to the physical body, all the memories and experiences inscribed in it from the life just lived become free. These vivid, fast-moving images surround the deceased like an animated film and reveal to them the totality of their earthly life. Events dating back to their earliest childhood, conscious and unconscious deeds, even forgotten incidents and overlooked events now appear in this sequence of images. The person's consciousness expands to the extent that they are present in each of these life scenes; at the same time, they see these experiences from the perspective of an objective observer.

This life-review or panorama is often described in near-death experiences, when the etheric body becomes partially detached from the physical body. One of the interviews in my near-death study described this process as follows:

There was a flood of light. I don't want to say it came
from a particular source; there was just this light,
flowing through the whole space. And connected with

it was a feeling of reality that I had never experienced before. I felt as though I was *really seeing* for the first time, as if all that I had thought of before as seeing didn't deserve the name. I saw my whole life then. It was all there, every detail, and all at the same time. I realised that everything had been right, and in that moment I was filled with an indescribable joy at this beautiful life. At the same time there was a feeling of deep sadness and regret about the many useless and unnecessary efforts with which I had tormented myself and other people, to put things in order, ignorant that they were all right long ago. It was also clear to me that time as a concept perhaps only holds true within a very small frame of reference, but beyond that, it's no longer valid. I believe we have the choice of staying within time or outside time, that is, in the present. This feeling of timelessness or of the moment, of the present . . . all this came from looking back on life.

Another interviewee had a near-death experience during a heart attack. He described looking back on his life in great detail:

It began when I had the sweat outbreak [meaning his heart attack], and then it went backwards, through every event to when I came into the world. I was an abrupt birth; I knew that from my mother, but I couldn't imagine what that was, an abrupt birth. I saw my mother sitting there with my father kneeling in front of the bed. He was waiting for me. I could see him sitting there with open arms. And then, in a matter of seconds, I was there, I saw my father receiving me into his arms.

47

He gave further details of his life review; I offer a short extract from it here:

> I saw pictures from my life. If it was a good deed, a good picture, the whole thing looked bright; if the intention wasn't good, it was like a dark dent, an indentation, do you know what I mean? I saw how I made out with girls as a young boy, forgive me, you know what I mean, don't you? I mean, that was nothing bad, but as a young lad you like to fool around with girls, and you make promises you don't keep because you want to get something from them. You understand what I mean, don't you? Young boys do that sometimes, when they want something from girls, and that's what I did there. I didn't always do something, sometimes it was just an intention, but that was there too, it appeared as a dark picture.

'You mean that not only your negative deeds but also your negative intentions appeared dark to you?' I asked.

'Yes, exactly.'

For everyone who has this experience, the accumulated impression of their life, which they experience as both spectator and actor, and through which they perceive the meaning of their actions and intentions, is a disturbingly deep insight into their life. Here the deceased is confronted with all the facets of their former life in such a way that nothing is embellished or falsified: all self-deception and insincerity falls away. The distinction between 'good' and 'bad' is not imposed upon us from without in the form of an external judgement; instead the person experiencing it evaluates the events of their life themselves. The beautiful and the good fill them with a light-filled joy;

the unpleasant they experience as an oppressive, shameful or frightening burden.

It can be difficult for us to grasp how an extremely complex, temporally dynamic and life-encompassing panorama can be perceived all at once and in such detail. It also seems a contradiction that we can be both the one experiencing an event and the one observing it.

The physical world is the world of separateness, so the fact that the deceased can perceive the people they have left behind parallel to experiencing their retrospective is another aspect that breaks through our physical integration into time and space.

A young man in a comatose state, who was inwardly deciding whether to remain in the spiritual world or to return to earth, described his experiences afterwards:

> I perceived how many people thought of me during this time. I felt that my whole family had prayed for me and that their love was helping me. This love worked like waves, like vibrations, like pulsations that did me good. They definitely had a healing effect on my condition. I also saw how some people lit candles for me in church, people I would not have expected such behaviour from. Even people I had thought badly of before now were thinking of me. I felt that all of this was doing me good, that it was having a healing effect on my condition.

A person living in the etheric world not only has insights into earthly life, they also perceive the thoughts and feelings of those left behind. They feel the grief of family and friends; they feel their kind thoughts and prayers, which give them light and warmth. In the same way, they also perceive their negative thoughts, which grieve and burden the person in the etheric world. The connection with those who were inwardly close is still powerful. Consequently, we on earth bear responsibility for all that we bring to the deceased during this time.

It also happens far more frequently than is assumed that a deceased person appears to their relatives or friends in the first days after crossing the threshold. This presence can occur spontaneously and unexpectedly in everyday situations. The intense feeling of a presence in the room arises and what emanates from the deceased becomes perceptible. Usually, such experiences are connected with a sense of peace, inner warmth and love. For many people, the certainty arises that the deceased lives on after death. Others, on the other hand, shy away from such perceptions or do not allow them at all because they do not correspond to their own ideas about death. A negative attitude in the bereaved is painful for the deceased because they want to communicate something or express a request. Here is an example.

For a brief time in the clinic, I looked after a young patient, barely in her mid-thirties, who had severe lung disease. She was married and mother to a four-year-old daughter. She could no longer get out of bed. Breathing was only possible with the help of oxygen; speaking took significant effort. From a medical point of view, a lung transplant was her last chance. She was on the transplant list, waiting, hoping and afraid. Her condition deteriorated and she knew that her life was hanging by a thread. Some days she thought about dying. Other days she was afraid and did not want to leave her daughter behind.

During our last therapeutic conversation, she told me about a dream she'd had the night before. She was sitting on a beautiful, big tree swing. On a majestic green branch behind her stood her angel, who encouraged her to swing higher. She asked me what the dream could mean. Although I had some idea,

I didn't want to give her a ready-made answer. I tried to create a space for her to talk, where she could deal with the images and feelings of the dream herself. At first, she was afraid that the dream might predict her death, then she tried to reinterpret it as an expression of her recovery. I could clearly feel that she was struggling inside and was not yet ready to die. I concluded our conversation with the words: 'Either way, you can trust your angel to be with you. He gives you courage.'

'Courage yes, but for what?'

'That will soon become clear; have confidence.'

I did not see her after that because she was transferred to another clinic. About ten days later she died before the hoped-for lung transplant could take place.

After her death this patient appeared to me as an etheric spirit figure. She seemed quiet, weak and sad. The light shining from her was dull. I asked her what I could do for her. At first, she did not answer. I asked her again and waited patiently, then she said timidly:

'Nobody lights a light for me, nobody.'

'Do you mean a candle? Your family doesn't light a candle for you? Not even your parents?'

'No, they don't believe that I still exist. I stand beside them, and they do not see me. They never look.'

'And your husband?'

'He does not know how to deal with it. He suppresses it. Everyone takes care of the little one and tries to suppress it. Everyone looks away from me. They are afraid to think of me, to see me.'

'If I can, I will gladly help you. What do you need? What can I do?'

'Could you just light a candle for me? That would be enough.'

I promised her I would do this for as long as she needed. From then on, I lit a candle for her every evening and said a prayer. After about two months she appeared again, but this time she did not seem as deeply depressed. She thanked me in her quiet manner and said it had helped her. She no longer needed the candlelight; she could go further into the light herself from now on. We said goodbye to one another and she left the etheric world.

The first period after death is a time of looking back on our life, of letting go and saying farewell to beloved people and places. Some deceased people feel liberated right away: they experience harmony and light. Others, however, still need care, support and help from those they've left behind. Warmth of heart, sincere affection, and loving and luminous thoughts are helpful and invigorating for every deceased person in the etheric world.

6

At Our Own Funeral

Oh, do not grieve!
Though you are not with me
One light we are
And it shines from me to you.

Christian Morgenstern, 'Oh, Do Not Grieve'

During the time when the deceased is still close to the earth in the etheric world, their funeral takes place. In European cultures of earlier times, burials took place three days after death. Incorporated into this custom was the old mystery knowledge that the etheric body remains close to the physical body for three days after death. Then the etheric body expands into the etheric world and the deceased continues on into the soul world and then into the spirit world. The funeral was not only a farewell to the corpse, to the earthly part of the deceased, but also to their etheric body. The physical body and the etheric body, the two lower members of the human being, had together formed the framework of the earthly incarnation. Now they separate from the higher members of the human being, the soul body and the 'I', which are released into their spiritual home.

In our time, funerals no longer take place three days after

death, but mostly a little later. External, organisational factors are considered rather than the spiritual path of the deceased. However, this need not be a cause for concern, since the time sequences for the deceased have also become very individualised. With many, we can notice that the detachment and expansion of their etheric body does indeed take place somewhat later.

Strange as it may sound, the deceased always attend their funeral. The presence of the mourning community is a strong focus for them. They perceive the feelings and emotions of the bereaved and experience the funeral service intensively. Through the presentation of their biography, they once again perceive their former path of destiny in a condensed form and at the same time see it through the eyes of others. How the deceased approach this event is often quite individual and varied.

One day I was at the funeral of a former colleague. The lady had worked until her seventieth year. She was a cheerful, humorous and remarkably positive person. She was a motherly type, compassionate and helpful. Her spirit was open and receptive to everything spiritually Christian. She viewed growing older without fear and often talked about death like a good friend. I liked her very much and still had sporadic contact with her after her retirement. As time passed, her health deteriorated and after two strokes she became bedridden. But even in this weakened state and through all her physical suffering, her positivity and optimism remained.

When she died, I went to her funeral, which she had meticulously planned months before with her children. She had written down her life story for the priest; she had chosen the music and had also named the people she wanted to be present. Arriving at the chapel, I took a seat in a back row. The room was full. Her children and grandchildren were sitting in front; it was a big family. Many of her acquaintances and friends were present and it was impressive to see that all these people were connected with the deceased in sincere love and friendship. It is not a matter of course to leave behind such traces of our life. The atmosphere in the room was very moving. I tried to sense whether the deceased was present but could not at first perceive anything. Then the music began to sound, an orchestral suite by Bach which had been her favourite piece. The music filled the room and almost all those present began to cry. I tried with all my strength to suppress my tears, but I hardly succeeded. Suddenly, I heard the voice of the deceased close to me, in her very trustworthy, cordial way: 'It's nice that you play my favourite Bach, but you don't all have to cry about it! I am here! My dear, you, at least, stop!'

I was so surprised by this unexpected interlude that I had to laugh. It was really her, with her typical way of speaking, her humour and spontaneity. I could not yet see her, but I felt her presence moving through the ranks of mourners. After a while, when the music had faded, she appeared in front of the priest. From there, she filled the room with love and sent a ray of light to each person present. The atmosphere was beautiful and dignified. But when the priest began to read her life story, and the people were once more close to tears, I heard her speak again: 'Father, as beautiful as your reading is, you don't need to emphasise everything so much. People are crying again. If I had known how maudlin everyone would be today, I would have written it less pregnant with meaning.' Again, her wit and humour lit up. After her death, her inner being radiated just what had distinguished her all her life: compassion and empathy, understanding for others and positivity in every situation.

At a completely different funeral, a young man, a former school friend of mine, who was thirty-seven years old, had died in a climbing accident in the mountains. He left behind his young wife, his three-year-old son and his mother, with whom he had had a very close relationship. He had been a very gentle person, loved and appreciated by all. His death came as a terrible blow to everyone, and now at his funeral there were hundreds of young people – school and college friends, colleagues – who were all devastated that he had been taken in the prime of life. The pain and shock filled the chapel.

As the funeral began, I tried to focus on my spiritual surroundings and eventually I was able to perceive the deceased young man. He floated above the crowd, spread out over the whole room. He radiated a deep peace and seemed very relaxed and carefree. The funeral itself did not interest him very much. Instead he tried to alleviate the pain of those present with his love. I greeted him inwardly and spoke to him.

'My friend, why did you die? Why now in particular?'

'That was enough for me,' he answered cheerfully. 'I did not want to achieve more in this life. I had no other plans for this time; everything I had planned before my birth was there. It was a full life.'

'But your son is so small; now he has to grow up without you.'

'No, I am still with him, only in another form. I will always accompany him. It was agreed between the two of us. Before he came to earth, he already knew that we would only meet here for a short time; we had both agreed to that much earlier. That is enough for what he needs in this life. I am not gone; I will always look after him.'

'For your mother, for your wife, the loss is also very great.'

'Their paths continue; their loss has meaning for both of them. Right now there is the pain, but if you look at the whole thing, it is right. For me it's right.'

'And why did you die that way? In the mountains? By falling?'

'It was actually a very beautiful death. When I fell, I was

already free. I did not feel anything, only that I floated over the world, and it was wonderful. It also has a meaning for the mountain. My life forces have remained there, they belong to it.'

'And now? How are things to go on? Do you need something from us? Can I do something for you?'

'No, I am fine, I am free and can go on from here. From this life I take forces that will help me in my next life. Next time I will come with more strength.'

That is how we said farewell. Meanwhile, the funeral continued. His little son, who had slept in his pushchair until then, woke up in the middle of it. He looked around and saw the many people in this unfamiliar room. Suddenly, something on the ceiling seemed to attract his attention. He looked up and began to beam. His face shone; he gurgled and rejoiced. The people around him shook their heads with pity and whispered: 'Look, the poor little one, he can't understand what's happening here. He doesn't even know that his papa died.' I closed my eyes and saw that the little boy was able to perceive his father spiritually, who at this very moment was hovering over the whole room. The child was pleased; they exchanged ideas and their hearts were lovingly connected. Of course, the child could not understand that he was at his father's funeral. But he could experience him spiritually. Children can often perceive angels, deceased human beings and elemental beings.

The presence of the deceased can therefore always be expected at the funeral. However, this happens in quite different intensities and moods. Some deceased people spread radiantly over the entire group of mourners, enveloping the events and those present with warmth and love. They listen carefully to what is said, perceiving in detail the depictions of their biography and the inner emotions of the participants. Some bring a bit of humour with them and are anxious to make the mood more cheerful. Others become aware that they have left behind unresolved circumstances or family burdens. They are restless and depressed. There are also deceased people who have not realised that they have died and therefore do not understand that they are now attending their own funeral. They are amazed at what is happening and do not understand why people are talking about them but do not notice them. Some even grumble about the priest's address, are piqued by the statements of individual members or by the presence of certain mourners.

The quite different and sometimes astonishing experiences we can have reflect both the most characteristic traits of the deceased person and their current inner state. A person does not become another person overnight after their death. Their character traits, thoughts and feelings still correspond very strongly to their previous state. The soul lives on and with it everything that made it what it was. A loving, compassionate, open-hearted person remains so after their death. In the same way, a distrustful, dissatisfied, negative person retains many of these qualities after death. Even if they now recognise and regret many things in the broader context of their life, they are not immediately a transformed human being.

Time spent in the etheric world is only an intermediate stage between the earthly world and the higher worlds of soul and spirit. Many people who have died succeed in making this transition in a quick and wonderfully sublime way. But there are many others who struggle to detach themselves from their old habits and patterns of thought, and who thus experience great difficulty in turning their attention away from the earth towards the higher spiritual world.

7

Caught Between Worlds

Everything you hold, you are held by,
And where you rule, you are the servant.
Pleasure sees itself separate from need,
And a duty attaches to every right.

Only what you reject can come back to you.
What you disdain approaches, eternally coaxing,
And in parting, taken from possessions,
You receive what is yours alone: You!

Franz Grillparzer, 'Renunciation'

Human development is becoming more individualised in all areas of life. In the same way that earthly biographies increasingly emancipate themselves from traditional contexts and assume a completely independent character, so has progress in the afterlife also become increasingly individualised. The growth and development of the human being has been transferred more firmly into the sphere of their personal freedom, not only in earthly life but also after death. Hence, they now bear responsibility for their progress in the spiritual spheres as well.

In earlier times primarily the angels were entrusted with the task of guiding the progression of the dead. Figuratively speaking, we could say that the guardian angels took the deceased with them after their physical death and led them, step by step, through the etheric world, soul world and spirit world. Of course, the deceased went through individual experiences concerning themselves, but they perceived their guardian angel more directly as a spiritual guide and lived more strongly in the feeling of being enveloped and led by them. Accordingly, their path through the afterlife took a more general course, at least as a rule. The angel's hand guided and conducted the transition from one spiritual level to the next.

This has changed, however, with the beginning of a new stage in the spiritual evolution of humankind. It is now increasingly humanity's responsibility consciously and independently to carry out the developmental steps in the life after death. The human being must also *want* to walk this path. The angels continue to help the deceased, but they no longer appear as guides; instead, they have become the companions and attendants of human beings.

For progress to take place in the spiritual spheres, there must be a voluntary and active impetus for development within the individual human soul. In our time, however, numerous people cross the threshold completely unprepared. They have no conceptions or ideas about what awaits them, and after death they are disoriented and insecure. Others are unwilling to let go of earthly conditions: they struggle to accept that things having to do with the material world, for example, possessions, power, claims, expectations, worries and obligations, are no longer relevant after death. They continue to cling to their earthly circumstances and do not open their consciousness up to the spiritual planes that now surround them. Then there are those who are so frightened by their life review that they feel only shame, dismay, or horror. They are overwhelmed by this unexpected self-image and do not consider themselves worthy to proceed further into the light.

Just as any incarnated person can miss a step in their development, bypass a process, or overlook an opportunity in any phase of their biography, so too is it possible for a deceased soul not to take some steps immediately because they remain trapped in a particular state of consciousness. If we look at the etheric aura of any city in the developed world, we will notice that in countless houses, among many other beings, there are the spiritual figures of deceased people. Our world is teeming with them. The appearance and concerns of the deceased who have remained trapped in this way vary considerably. Their length of stay in this intermediate world can also vary between a few days, several decades, or hundreds of years. Because they have not discarded their etheric body, they appear to the spiritual eye in quite clear contours, in a form that still resembles their former physical self. Many of them wander in the earth-bound sphere without having contact with their angel, who is nevertheless always with them.

These deceased people who have become trapped always have a focus, a point of reference towards which they orient themselves. They may be drawn to the aura of a living human being and influence that person's thoughts and feelings and even their actions. The deceased soul wants to impose their own impulses or problematic issues on this person. They also draw on the spiritual powers of the besieged person, draining their energy. In such cases, we speak of 'possession'.

Other deceased persons who remain trapped in the etheric are caught in certain places they cannot let go of, for example in the spiritual environs of their former home, workplace, or accident site. They burden the atmosphere of these places with their unsolved problems, which continue to exert an influence in that space. Here, too, we can speak of a 'possession', because what happens there is influenced by the deceased.

Possession by the dead who have remained trapped happens far more frequently than most people assume. Each case is individual and the reasons for it are manifold. However, we can identify typical characteristics and classic patterns that lead to this phenomenon.

Traumatic death

We have already described how a sudden or violent death can come as such a shock for the deceased person that at first they cannot understand what is happening. In the incarnated state, extreme shock often leads to a person becoming traumatised, they are unable to process the terrible event. The person's being is partially torn apart and the upper members of the human being can no longer intervene appropriately to exert their healing, harmonising effect.

A sudden or violent death can have an even more pronounced effect. The soul is not prepared to leave the body, as is the case in a natural, more gradual dying process, but instead is torn from it. The lowest member of the deceased person is now their etheric body. This is remarkably similar in form and closely connected to the physical body and so it is not immediately clear to the deceased person that a momentous change has taken place. They may find themselves hovering above the scene of their death, even though this is not natural in the physical state. They may also be surprised that no one notices them or talks to them any more, but their confusion is so great that they do not necessarily draw clear conclusions from such perceptions.

The deceased person, in a state of deep shock, now clings to their etheric body as they used to cling to their physical body and continues to focus all their attention on the familiar earthly world. It can happen that such deceased people wander about in this state for a long time. Some of them remain at the place of death and experience the shocking event repeatedly. Psychologically, this condition would be described as post-traumatic stress disorder. On highways and streets, there are many places where such deceased persons drift around in their life bodies. The energies of such sites become burdened and accidents can occur at just those places because the deceased continue to relive their accidents. These are classic examples of possessed places.

It is understandable that relatives place crosses and flowers at the site of a loved one's fatal accident, but for those who died there this gives no help. The site of the accident becomes a kind of shrine that attracts the deceased person and strengthens their attachment to the place even more. This custom has another adverse effect: through the symbols of mourning that are placed there, through the feelings and thoughts of the bereaved, which are uniquely connected to this place, they put the stamp of an accident on the place and consolidate the negative energy there. It therefore makes no sense – neither for the dead nor for the location – to maintain these as memorial sites over extended periods.

Of course, not all the dead remain in the location where they died in a state of shock. Many of them seek out more familiar places, which in their disoriented state can give them a sense of stability and security. In most cases, this is their own home. They return in their disembodied form and to begin with everything is good again: they are in familiar settings, surrounded by familiar objects and family members. This has a calming effect on their desolate condition.

Of course, they notice that other people no longer react to them, which surprises them at first. They may become desperate or angry and this can express itself as noises, knocks or footsteps that are not produced by the physical people in the house. These are the bundled energies that emanate from the deceased, and whilst they cannot usually work their way into the physical plane, the elemental beings present react to them in a way that can be heard physically. Many ghosts and the stories told about them can be traced back to this phenomenon, but such events are rare exceptions. As a rule, the deceased who remain in the etheric are not physically perceptible.

Over time, these deceased come to terms with their new condition. They still do not understand why no one pays them any attention, but at the same time they don't know what else to do but to accept the situation as it is. Their consciousness is still subdued, their attention narrowly focused on this particular place. They lead a parallel existence to the people whose earthly lives take place in the same location. Such deceased do not lift their gaze to the spiritual world, which means that the light of their consciousness is not strong enough to orient themselves away from earthly connections. Mostly they perceive neither their guardian angel nor other spiritual entities, and when they notice a known deceased who tries to make contact, they are frightened and turn away from them.

For many of the deceased, this condition can extend over very long periods, and only a change of consciousness makes their emancipation from this intermediate world possible. Here is an example.

A kindergarten teacher once asked for my help. She explained that some of the rooms in the kindergarten had a very oppressive atmosphere and that in these rooms there was a striking amount of discord, both among the teachers and between teachers and parents. This was not the case, however, in other rooms in the kindergarten and among other groups. She had also recently noticed that a memorial stone had been placed in front of the house in memory of a Jewish woman deported and murdered by the Nazis. The teacher herself was able, albeit slightly, to sense subtle psychic energies in her environment, and she had the impression that there might be a connection.

I agreed to help and went along to the kindergarten. The house itself was well looked after and lovingly furnished, but the atmosphere was dark and heavy. It was located in a place that seemed to be wounded from times far in the past. I saw visions of animals being slaughtered and later of people who had been murdered there. The earth had been soaked with blood, and the desperate cries of the victims had been embedded in the memory of the place. It was necessary therefore to purify this place.

As we began our work, I saw the figure of a petite, elderly lady. She was well groomed and wore old-fashioned clothes. I began a conversation with her and realised that this was the woman for whom the memorial stone had been erected. She was in a state of distress: feelings of indignation and powerlessness continually rose up within her as she repeated the same sentences over and over. Gradually I was able to learn her story. She had lived in this house during her lifetime, renting a room there in order to be close to her sister-in-law, who lived a few houses away in a Jewish old people's home. The lady's husband had died years before. One night she was picked up by the Gestapo and deported via Theresienstadt to an extermination camp in Belarus. When she arrived she was so weak that she was shot at once.

The shock of the deportation had been too much for her. When the Gestapo had burst into her apartment she had hidden in the closet, terrified, but the soldiers had found her and dragged her out. The trauma of that experience, and the outrageous sense of injustice done to her, had overwhelmed her ability to deal with it. Even before her death, she had become so emotionally disturbed that her 'I' had detached itself from the reality of her situation: her arrest in the middle of the night, the long and terrible train journey and her execution at the end of it, all seemed to her like a nightmare. She had not understood that she had died, and after her death she had returned home to her familiar place as an etheric figure. There she had waited for more than seventy years, in the place where the drama of her death had begun.

Unable to overcome what was done to her, the lady remained trapped in her anger and entirely fixated on this place. It would not have occurred to her to leave. She wanted an apology for the affront she had suffered, and for the events of that night to be undone. She was oblivious to how her negative energies affected the atmosphere of the house, and only as if in a dream was she aware of other people coming and going. Their presence in the house was of no significance to her. Instead her inner life circled endlessly around the same traumatic event.

It was not easy to explain to her the damage she was doing and how she was burdening people who had nothing to do with her story. I said that it was natural for her to feel that these terrible events had devalued her life, and that it was also natural to want understanding and recognition. But those involved at that time had long since died. She could no longer do or achieve anything in this earthly place. After two long and very intense sessions, her state of mind changed. She very much regretted burdening the children and the people working there; that had never been her intention. She understood that she had to leave, even though it was not easy for her. But with the help of several angelic beings, and in the presence of her long-deceased relatives who had been waiting for her all this time, she was finally able to depart.

The atmosphere in the kindergarten improved significantly after this work. Yet not all difficulties were resolved. The house, as already mentioned, remained burdened on other levels, and the people who worked there contributed their own personal and unresolved problems too. But at least the level that had been occupied by the deceased lady was now free and no longer gave rise to such a fundamental mood of discord.

This incident is by no means an exception. Repeatedly I meet the deceased from the time of the World Wars who have not yet left the earthly sphere. Some of them still appear to the mind's eye as if they were wearing the uniform of that time, a sure sign that they are still in the life realm or etheric world closest to the earth. Some of them have remained trapped by a sense of their own victimhood: they can neither forgive nor cope with their terrible experiences. Others were perpetrators: they are plagued by their conscience and cannot forgive themselves. Many are both and experience themselves torn apart in an unresolvable conflict between victim and perpetrator.

Such tragic destinies still affect our world and show that traumatising experiences can have an effect not only in the days and weeks after a person's death, but also over more extended periods.

Taking mind-altering medication

As already described in connection with crossing the threshold, not only can terrible experiences and violent causes of death mean that a person does not correctly perceive the moment of their own passing, but the intake of various painkillers or mind-altering drugs in the time before death can also result in the deceased remaining in a dulled state of consciousness.

A therapist friend of mine asked me for help with one of his patients, a young woman who had been in biographical counselling with him for a year. She was twenty-four years old and had cancer. A year later he found out that she had died after an extended stay in hospital. He continued to think about her and felt impelled to ask me if she might need help.

I directed my inner attention towards her and perceived her as a beautiful, elegant but very sad figure. She was in a dim state of awareness and appeared as though she was floating alone in a greyish sphere, completely isolated from her surroundings. She didn't really know what was happening to her, and although she suspected that she had died, her lethargic condition had left her trapped in this intermediate space. Conversation with her was difficult: she seemed very absent-minded, but I was able to understand from this that her death had been a very painful experience. Her cancer had metastasised, and despite the medication she had suffered massive pain. Emotionally she seemed to regret losing her young life, although she did not struggle very much with it. Overall, she gave the impression of one who had been largely absent in the last period of her life and who now, after crossing the threshold, had remained in this shadowy condition.

Since her state of consciousness did not allow for a very clear exchange of ideas that could have helped her, I used a different method. On the spiritual level, it is possible to convey information by way of forces connected with the heart without having to explain the relevant content thought by thought or word by word. Because our brain is no longer in the way, a direct transmission of ideas is possible. We can bundle complex connections together and make them immediately available to another being. I created a similar bundle containing all of my inner knowledge about the spiritual world and asked the young woman to let it work on her heart.

The young woman took up this content. At first she was quite astonished by it because her own inner images about death and the spiritual world were vague and uncertain, but gradually her awareness began to clear. I was then able to turn her attention to her angel and towards the deceased relatives surrounding her. With the help of these beings, she was able to leave this intermediate sphere and turn towards the soul world.

A strongly subdued state of consciousness before death can lead to inner apathy and immobility after death. Those affected lack the mental alertness to perceive the reality of the etheric world surrounding them and to be active within it. They persist in the belief that they are still bound to a sick or aching body, a lingering impression from their former physical body that determines their consciousness. In houses that were inhabited for a long time by bedridden people, in old people's homes and in nursing homes, I often meet deceased people who continue to live there. In hospitals, such deceased persons who are not yet aware of their death still drift around disoriented, although they do not usually stay there for long periods since hospitals are not as familiar to them as home.

Addictive behaviour and drug-related death

In addition to the effects of medications that alter consciousness, intoxication and drug use can also obscure the moment of death. In an intoxicated state, as is the case with severe alcohol poisoning or the influence of drugs, the limits of reality become blurred. The 'I' is no longer master in its own house and the state of consciousness is deeply clouded. A person who has died in this way does not necessarily perceive their detachment from the physical body. Moreover, their habits and desires are still present. They are trapped in their addiction and go in search of its satisfaction: they often gravitate to the drug or alcohol milieu and cling to living addicts in order to get to the desired substance through them. Their desire, which they can never fulfil because they lack a physical body, drives them to continually encourage the person they occupy in their addictive behaviour. To have such an addicted deceased person as 'baggage' means that the possessed person's own addiction intensifies. This also explains why alcohol and drug withdrawal are so difficult: addicts fight – not always, but very often – not only their own addiction but also the influence of deceased persons who want to satisfy their craving through them.

For the deceased, the issue of addiction not only plays a crucial role in the etheric world, because addictions and dependencies also have a considerable effect on the deceased person's experience in the soul world.

Chemotherapy and its possible consequences

Chemotherapy can also have a pronounced effect on a person's time in the etheric world. This is not about a limited state of consciousness that makes the transition more difficult, but about the impact that the administered substances have on the physical and etheric bodies of the person concerned. Chemotherapy can lead to a drastic hardening of the etheric body and cause it to bind strongly to the physical body. After death, this tenacious etheric body does not adapt properly to its environment. It takes longer to soften and lighten so that it can disperse, thereby allowing for the transition of the deceased person into the soul world. Depending on the form and duration of the chemotherapy, it can take between a few weeks to several months until the consequences of this treatment have subsided.

These observations do not speak against chemotherapy. We should, however, be aware of the effects on the etheric level that need to be either treated or else tolerated by the affected person.

Being bound to the here and now

Some deceased persons find it difficult to detach themselves from specific earthly contexts. Life and relationship issues, concern for partners, children, houses or property, emotional dependence, or supposed personal or professional obligations occupy these people to such an extent that they cannot or do not want to get rid of them. The assumed problem absorbs all their attention so that the spiritual events around them are entirely eclipsed. Most of the time, and often without noticing it, they occupy a specific habitat or cling to the aura of a relative. Instead of contributing to the desired solution to a problem, they become a burden.

Several years ago, my husband and I spent our summer holidays in Norway. We had rented a small house near the beach, surrounded by meadows and forest. The two-storey house was old but beautifully maintained and full of charm. Externally, everything was enchanting, but the atmosphere there was at times oppressive. One night I was lying in bed reading when it seemed to me that a sinister figure was standing in front of the window and gesticulating. Since fear is not a good starting point for spiritual work, I spoke the Lord's Prayer to calm and centre myself. Then I turned to this spirit figure who hovered in the darkness in front of the bedroom window. He was an angry old man, who scolded furiously and made threatening gestures. The deceased was tall and robust. His figure was reminiscent of a Norwegian farmer at the beginning of the twentieth century and his character was quite coarse and sullen. He could not see his angel standing behind him. His eyes were always on the house.

I began a conversation with him. I learned that during his lifetime he had built this house by himself, which had involved significant effort. He had spent his whole life here, and after death he could not let go of it because this was his entire world. He had the impression that he had to take care of it and protect it and so he remained close by. He couldn't understand why strangers were continually coming into his house, why they lived there and left again, and how all this could happen without his permission. He was furious about it and rumbled around like an angry Rumpelstiltskin. He was by no means an evil figure, merely a bitter, troubled old man who had remained trapped, unable to separate himself from his earthly possessions.

I turned to his angel and asked him to make his relationships clearer to me. The angel showed me in pictures that the descendants of this man had partly used the house themselves after his death, but then left it uninhabited for a long time. The following generation, which had no connection to it, had renovated it and rented it out as a holiday home. The old man, who had neither understood that he was no longer alive nor that this was no longer his house, could not cope with the situation and remained there, scolding and raging.

It was no easy task to convey to this man that he no longer lived in the earthly world. He was quite simple-minded, and after eighty years it was difficult to persuade him to move away from there. I tried it step by step. First, I pointed out to him that he could float and that he was standing outside in front of a window on the second floor. Then I asked him to come into the house, which he did, and I told him that he had entered through the wall and not the door. His dulled consciousness now began to wonder. Even though he could not explain it, he was at least beginning to question his circumstances. I made contact with him again the next day. I encouraged him to rise high above the village and look out over the landscape: first Norway and then the whole of Europe. Eventually, he realised he was no longer incarnated and he now became more open and inwardly mobile. He became aware of his angel, and was very moved. He could also see his mother, who had died long before him and who wanted to help him on his journey. The man remained uncertain, but he was at least ready to follow his spiritual companions and leave this place.

Bondage to specific earthly situations is a recurring theme. In such cases the deceased person lacks the confidence that life on earth can continue without them. For example, the head of a business, whose entire life was his company, would still 'go to work' every day because he refused to accept that he had died. During his lifetime he had identified himself so completely with his work that he could not now let go of it: he was disturbed to find another person sitting in his chair in his office making decisions. In order to put things back to the way they were when he was alive, he repeatedly tried to undermine everything new. His negative energies created complications and difficulties, weakening the further development of the company.

Not only possessions and claims to power, but all of the dead's unresolved negative emotions, such as anger, envy, resentment, jealousy and hatred represent a burden for the world of the living. For example, if a deceased person does not allow their husband or wife to have a new partner, they can obstruct any new relationship. Their jealousy and associated negative energies can place an increased burden on the new partnership, causing all manner of discontent and disputes to develop. The new couple are not even aware that there is a third person undermining their relationship.

The main problem with such unredeemed soul impulses is their persistence: the person creating them is trapped in them as in a spider's web. At the same time, they harm their victims because they continually burden them with uncontrolled, demanding or destructive claims. Some of these dead may even be aware that they have died, but that no longer interests them. Their main focus now is ending the unwanted situation.

There is only one sensible solution for this: to help the deceased make their way into the spiritual world. If they do not understand this, then they should be made to do so. Working through their unprocessed life issues does not mean allowing them to do so in such a destructive way. To retain a personal claim on the earthly world is selfish. Death has its meaning and its correctness, both for the deceased and for those they leave behind. For the deceased, their task now is to learn to let go and become acquainted with new dimensions of reality. If they do not keep to this spiritual order, then the responsibility for it passes to us.

How the bereaved affect the deceased

Although it is the task of each individual human being to shape their growth and development after death, they can be helped or hindered in this by very specific external influences. A person who has recently crossed the threshold is still connected to those they have left behind. They perceive the emotions of their relatives, their pain and grief.

Mourning is the sister of pain; it is an expression of loss that binds the mourner to something that existed in the past but which no longer exists in the same way in the present. Dealing with grief, allowing it, accepting it, giving it space and time is part of a healthy process of emotional development and healing. However, mourning has its foundations in different layers of the soul and can show itself in subtly different ways. We can, for example, mourn for someone who has died, but we can also mourn for ourselves. This difference often goes unnoticed. Behind the understandable pain of loss, there can also hide the desire to have the person who has crossed the threshold with you again. This implies, however, that we do not accept their death as part of our life. Here the border between genuine grief and egoism becomes quite porous.

The quality of mourning, therefore, plays a key role. If a person cannot cope with the loss and is so overwhelmed by the pain that they cling to the deceased, they can prevent them from leaving the etheric sphere. Such emotions claw at the deceased and hold them back. They feel torn between worlds, and experience this state as oppressive and painful.

The actual educational work here concerns the bereaved and not the deceased. Tending to them in their grief, we can convey to them that through their inner attitude they have a direct influence on the development of the person who has crossed the threshold. Over time it becomes clear that trusting and letting go are the best companions for a deceased person. The deceased in turn can be encouraged to continue their path and to have confidence in the wise guidance at work in the destiny of the bereaved.

Mutual constraint

However, there are also cases in which there is *mutual* adherence, albeit faint. This means that both the deceased *and* their relatives are in need of a common existence and cannot let go of each other. This can be seen in older married couples who have spent many decades together: after the death of one partner, they remain intensely focused on each other and continue to live together.

Often, one of the partners is emotionally needier than the other and so remains fixated on them; the other, in turn, feels this subconsciously and inwardly circles around their companion, full of sympathy. It may even be that one of the partners suffers from this unresolved connection but cannot free themselves from it. Some cases are very touching, because, especially on the part of the men, a quality of love and connectedness sometimes comes to light that was not apparent in life.

A friend told me that her grandmother noticed the presence of her grandfather who had died years before. Sometimes the grandmother even had the impression that her husband was holding her. This was neither frightening nor alarming for the grandmother, but it was strange and a bit wearing. I was asked if it would be possible to help in this situation.

I was given the name of the deceased grandfather and meditated on him. The name is an essential bridge to reach those deceased whom we do not know personally. There are many kinds of spiritual beings, and those of a more demonic nature can set us on the wrong track by impersonating someone they are not. If we do not thoroughly examine our spiritual vision, such beings have the opportunity to fool us, but if we ask them directly for their name, they cannot lie and impersonate someone else. This spiritual law is an inherently important protection in working with spiritual beings.

After I made sure that I had found the real grandfather, I tried to understand his situation. He appeared in his etheric body, sitting on the sofa in the living room gazing out. Because it was late at night, his wife was asleep. He seemed to know that he had passed away, but he did not quite want to admit it. He was clearly attached to his wife and had stayed in the house out of concern for her. He was open and friendly and we talked about his life.

As long as we spoke about earthly things, the conversation went smoothly, but he did not want to talk about spiritual conditions.

I tried to tell him that his angel was with him, but he refused to accept this. When I showed him my angel standing behind me, he still did not believe me. 'Anyone can say that that is an angel,' he said. 'It could be anyone.' I thought about how I could make progress with him, and I realised that his wife was the key. He had the strongest connection to her; anything to do with her touched him deeply, so I decided to show him his wife's angel. I asked him to go with me to where his wife was sleeping. Although he had not had a physical body for years, he moved through the house as if he were still old and frail – a typical sign of a deceased person who has become trapped. He led me into the bedroom where his wife was asleep. We stood next to the bed and I showed him his wife's angel at the head end. 'This is your wife's angel. He guards her and guides her. He is always with her and has always been with her, only you never noticed him. Your wife's angel was with both of you throughout your marriage.' This touched the grandfather very much; he could perceive the angel's devotion and was deeply moved by it. From then on it was possible for him to see his guardian angel, as well as his parents, who had now appeared even though they had died a long time before.

I tried to tell him that he could not help his wife from the etheric plane he was on. I also gave him a 'heart bundle' of everything I knew about the spiritual world. As these soul images worked in him he became very thoughtful. He contemplated them for a long time, saying repeatedly: 'This is not what we were taught in school, not even in church. We didn't know that; I didn't know that.' Despite being moved by these new insights he was not ready to leave. That would mean leaving his wife and he could not imagine going anywhere without her.

I then asked his wife to join me. Although her physical body was asleep in the bed, her soul-spiritual being was able to respond. It became clear that she too was still holding onto her husband and could not let him go. Due to their strong relationship and their reluctance to let go of each other, they had created the existing situation.

I did not force the grandfather to leave. It would not have accomplished much, not least because his wife would have drawn him back repeatedly. I merely said farewell to both of them with the suggestion that the circumstances could change at any time.

As this example shows, the mutual relationship between the living and the dead can cause the latter to remain close to the earth, but this condition need not be an oppressive or stressful one. Sometimes it is experienced as waiting for the other, or as being enmeshed with the other. Such connections are understandable, of course, but it does not make much sense if this state lasts for a long time. Both the deceased and the dependant are hindered in their development and have not yet learned to let go.

Materialistic and atheistic worldviews

Our attitude towards death and our ideas about it play a significant role at all levels of the afterlife. Materialistically minded people are convinced that death means the end of their existence. After crossing the threshold, however, they experience that their consciousness is not extinguished. They also still have a body, though of a slightly different kind. For them this is an unexpected and extremely perplexing state, which they cannot fit into their familiar categories of thinking. Their encounters with angelic beings and other deceased persons can produce helplessness, dismay and even fear.

According to the principle 'what cannot be is not allowed to be', the difficulty for such people is that they cannot admit what they are experiencing. They have formed concepts and ideas only in accordance with earthly conditions; the idea of a real and meaningful interplay between life and death has not taken root in them. They did not consider the existence of spiritual dimensions, nor did the inner image of their angel live in their hearts. They do not allow any other reality than the earthly one to enter their minds and so they continue to direct their gaze towards the earth. Since the unknown often generates fear, many such deceased people avoid directing their attention to the new, unexpected levels of their being.

Above all, these deceased persons need enlightenment and clarification. Employing vivid and even humorous experiences, we can help them come to terms with the new reality in which they now live. We can show them, for example, that in their present state they can float and walk through walls, or that they cannot pick up any physical object. In the beginning, they are astonished and disbelieving. Some even try to argue cleverly against their own experience, but after some demonstrations, all their materialistic theories are refuted. When they are ready to perceive their angel, they are usually willing to move on.

Fear of death

Like the denial of existence in the afterlife, the fear of death is also a hindrance, at least in the etheric sphere. Some people have a diffuse fear of the 'unknown', others of personal 'extinction'. More often, however, this is a morally conditioned or religiously indoctrinated fear: the fear of eternal darkness, fear of the devil, fear of being punished for our sins.

Fear paralyses the deceased. They close down internally

and prefer to remain unmoved and motionless in the face of the expected threat or punishment. Any new impressions, as well as encounters with spiritual beings, come towards them like a terrible danger. With some of these deceased persons, we notice how they shield their 'I' in order not to perceive anything any more. This is comparable to the ostrich tactic of sticking your head in the sand in the hope that the danger will somehow pass you by. Consequently, the deceased remain in a rigid, cramped state.

Religious passivity

Even widespread religious concepts, if accepted without reflection, can complicate our time in the etheric world immediately after death. Some religious people accept ideas given to them by the church, or some other religious authority, without really considering them as existential questions. They have not made these ideas their own; in many cases, they are merely a collection of very literal quotations: 'When I die, I will fall asleep and will be raised on the Day of Judgement.' However, death is not a sleep; quite the contrary, it is a state that requires the highest spiritual awareness. The fact that we undergo an active process of development after death is foreign to those people who cultivated a more passive attitude towards life after death. When faced with the reality of this, such deceased people are very insecure. 'That's not what we were taught,' they say, or: 'The teacher at school didn't say it would be like that,' or: 'The priest told us something different.' The spiritual passivity that was taught, as well as the lack of vitality in our faith, pose a special problem here.

Even such phrases as 'rest in peace' create false ideas of what the life after death is like. Behind this saying lies a deep wisdom, which was still known to people in earlier times. At that time, it was known that the deceased person, now in the soul world, was about to confront the totality of their soul life. This is often a painful, challenging experience and people would wish the dead person peace and calm in their confrontation with their own self. Over time, however, the knowledge of this connection was lost. All that remains of the original core of wisdom is an empty phrase that creates in many believers the general expectation of a state of passive acceptance in the hereafter.

Intellectual and dogmatic spiritual ideas

People who during their incarnation have developed very dogmatic spiritual views or fixed mental ideas about the spiritual world form a group of the deceased trapped in the etheric world who are seldom considered. In contrast to those who adopt ecclesiastical conventions of thought with little reflection, here we are dealing with people who are personally and consciously concerned with spiritual issues. However, they do so only in an intellectualised, opinionated and didactic way.

Dogmatism of any kind produces one-sided thoughts and inflexible inner images. Since the etheric body is the carrier of our ideas, rigid thought formations cause it to harden, meaning it then has difficulty dissolving after death. The solidity of the deceased's mental structures remains, leading them to confuse their own fixed ideas and imaginations with the actual spiritual world that now surrounds them. In such cases we find, for example, strongly intellectually inclined theosophists, hard-line esotericists or doctrine-oriented anthroposophists.

These deceased souls seek connections with living human beings who have a similar cast of mind and who generate comparable thought forms. For this reason, they are often found in theological seminaries, for example. Their focus is still on those places that formed the centre of their inner life. They continue to represent their ideas concerning the spiritual world and to influence the people working there in the formation of their own opinions and their need for recognition. This complicates the social structure in such institutions because thoughts and ideas of embodied people that differ from those of the deceased are regarded by the deceased as absurd and they fight against them. Out of spiritual dogmatism, real power struggles arise. In addition to this, there are beings of discord and strife who use the circumstances to intensify existing negative energies. They stir up chaotic states, deep-seated distrust, and ongoing disputes. The living people do not notice this consciously, but they are surprised by the huge social problems and complain about the unfortunate situation.

It is, therefore, a mistake to assume that those of the dead who have dealt with spiritual topics during their lifetime will easily act as 'helpers' for the earthly world. Spiritual thoughts alone do not guarantee a healthy development after death. Instead, emotional and spiritual mobility, tolerance and openness of heart are the prerequisites for an unbiased perception of the spiritual world and a harmonious development after death.

Suicide

Individual attention concerning development after death is necessary for people who have taken their own lives. Social opinions about suicide are deeply divided: on the one hand, suicide is regarded as a self-destructive act and condemned in the strongest terms; on the other hand, it is met with understanding and seen in the light of human self-determination.

Suicide is by no means a marginal phenomenon. Worldwide

nearly 800,000 people commit suicide each year, and for each successful attempt there are indications that more than twenty others have tried and failed to take their own life.[1] Additionally, there are unrecognised suicides such as unexplained road accidents, unnoticed discontinuation of essential medicines, and refusal of food in nursing homes, to give just a few examples. Statistically, about fifty per cent of suicide cases are related to depression, and another forty per cent to psychoses, addictions (alcohol and drug abuse) and sexual abuse. In the other ten per cent of cases, there are emotional states burdened by traumatic experiences or life crises.[2]

Behind each case lies a very individual fate, telling of pain and loss, loneliness and despair, fear and hopelessness. The reasons that lead to such an act are manifold and complex, but nearly all suicides have one thing in common: suicide is an existential act of desperation and as such bears the signature of a tragic life decision. Those affected find their situation hopeless and unbearable and see no other way out than to put an end to their existence.

When we accompany such a person beyond the threshold, we first perceive their horror at the fact that suicide has ended neither their existence nor their suffering. With dismay they realise that they have only destroyed their physical body; the problems they wanted to erase, along with the feelings that oppressed them, remain part of their existence. Deprived of their physical instrument, they cannot now intervene in their earthly development to change and reshape it.

So far, the experiences of nearly all those who commit suicide are the same. From here on, however, different realms of experience are created that determine the further development of the deceased soul after death.

Initially most suicides are trapped by the same feelings, fears and inner conflicts that preceded their death. The circumstances of their death, as well as the deed itself, are experienced over and over again. The shattering insight that there is now no turning back reinforces their sense of remorse and hopelessness. In addition, there are feelings of guilt over those they have left behind and a desire to reverse the suicide. They experience themselves trapped in a cocoon of constantly recurring thoughts and feelings, like some nightmarish psychological thriller in which the most terrible scenes are incessantly repeated.

A few years ago, I learned that an artist whom I had greatly admired had taken his own life. He had been a man in his prime, highly gifted, versatile and spirited. He was a remarkably sensitive person and had gone through several life crises, which had thrown him completely out of balance. Over time he became depressed, quarrelled with most people close to him and then one day violently ended his life.

I tried to perceive him spiritually and found him in a frightening state. He felt enclosed in total darkness and had the constant feeling of plunging into a bottomless abyss. He was surrounded by threatening demonic beings and he had the feeling of being continually torn apart. A shattering, ceaseless cry emanated from him. This scene was unbearable.

Conversation with him was not possible at that time, as his consciousness was imprisoned in that horrible scene, but I could perceive that he was accompanied inwardly by many people who prayed for him. He remained trapped for a long time, but at some point he began to perceive something of the loving gestures of those he had left behind. These gestures flowed into his destructive nightmare like tender streams of light and over the months they became a river that finally penetrated the darkness to his inner being.

In a later encounter with him, I could see that he had begun to notice the being of Christ shining behind this dark world. From then on, an active inner dialogue between light and darkness began in him. Although he still would not leave this sphere for some time, he had at least found a real guide outside his darkness.

After their suicides, many people find themselves confronted with similar terrible experiences. But suicides are by no means banished to a 'place of terror' from outside themselves, as is sometimes mistakenly assumed. It is their own state of mind that is reflected back to them: confusion, fear, self-reproach, shame and repentance torture them; they cannot forgive themselves, nor can they believe that they are entitled to forgiveness. At the same time, they shrink from the light-filled spirit beings who could help them.

There is also a group of suicides who do not notice that they have discarded their physical body. Since their confused and tormented state of mind continues after the act, they do not perceive that a change has taken place. The burning desire to put an end to it all is still with them and so they circle desperately in the maelstrom of their agonising soul experiences. Starting from the false idea that death must be the end of everything, they now fear other deceased or angelic beings and try to flee from them.

The support of relatives is a help and a comfort for all suicides. Yet it is not possible to lead them from the intermediate realm in which they find themselves as it is with other deceased souls in the etheric world. Often there are issues of possession, either by other deceased souls or by demon-like creatures who have drawn the suicide to them. To see through these possessions and to dissolve them is itself a task.

What can we do to help victims of suicide? First, we must love them without reproach and forgive them. This makes it easier for them to forgive themselves and to accept the love of the spiritual world. At the same time, however, it is crucial that they accept the consequences of their actions. They have to learn this lesson; any evasion only delays their further learning and development. A compassionate but firm and unsentimental approach is needed here so that the suicide victim can progress and not become a burden for their relatives.

Yet not all suicides have the same frightening experiences after crossing the threshold. Whilst it is painful for them to see the chances they have missed in the life just ended and they must also spend time in a gloomy, lonely world of their own making, still their experiences are not as terrifying or as tormenting as it is for others.

During my meditative work with suicides, I met Titus, a friendly soul who had left the earth a long time ago. In his past life he had been a young soldier who fought in a war. He was the last survivor of his battalion and the enemy was approaching. He was severely wounded and completely alone. He did not know what his captivity would be like: whether the enemy soldiers would torture him, kill him, or leave him alive. Believing that he was doing the honourable thing, he decided to take his own life, committing suicide in a quiet, dignified state of mind.

In flashback he showed me his experiences after crossing the threshold. He looked down on the battlefield and watched as the enemy soldiers searched the lifeless bodies of his comrades, one by one. Titus realised the soldiers were sorry to not find any survivors. They were not murderous. Indeed, it was a matter of honour for them to keep their enemies alive and take them as prisoners.

Titus remained with this troop of soldiers, accompanying them in spirit, and saw where he would have been taken as a prisoner. He realised that his life there would have given him tasks that would have allowed him to acquire new skills and abilities. In captivity, he would have experienced a humility that would have decisively shaped and changed his soul configuration. He would have encountered a new culture, with its unique customs and traditions, and in this way he would have enriched his understanding of the world. Over time his captivity would have been relaxed and he would have gained an entirely new experience of freedom. Titus became aware that through his suicide he had lost a valuable life, rich in experience. A deep sorrow lay on his soul.

His spirit always returned to the battlefield, to the place where he had died. There he mourned the loss of his earthly life. In general, he remained very attached to this place. From there he repeatedly followed the traces of his unlived life on earth. A few years later he would have met and married a certain young woman. Titus realised they had planned a life together before this incarnation, but now this could not take place. Unconsciously the young woman waited for him, and in her soul, though barely noticeable, there resonated a quiet mourning for this unfulfilled life. There were also two unborn souls who would have belonged to this family. Now this possibility of incarnation had been denied to them and they had to give their destiny a completely different form.

Everything Titus first experienced after death was infused with the painful feeling of what was not lived, of what was neglected. This did not solely affect him; his voluntary death had decisive consequences for the people linked by destiny with him. But despite his severe and profound regret, his soul experience was neither agitated nor agonising. He was not trapped in a nightmare. His development consisted of weighty cognitive processes that profoundly shaped him.

Spiritual work with suicides shows that the proportion of those who must walk a challenging path after death predominates. I have never experienced a suicide that was 'easy' in the afterlife. The person affected must always endure stressful and difficult states of mind. But the qualitative difference in experience can be very great. Over time, I have become aware that there are some essential building blocks to the event that decisively shape the post-death experience.

Our emotional condition prior to death significantly colours our experience after death. It is therefore decisive which forces (and thus which spiritual beings) dominate our soul experience. Not only do mental and emotional states persist after death, they also determine the nature of the particular act of suicide. The act can be violent and destructive, or it can be sluggish and resigned. There is a difference between whether a person kills themselves with a knife or takes tablets whilst lying quietly on the sofa. There is no 'better' or 'worse' way to commit suicide as far as being responsible for our life is concerned. But the *inner soul gesture* of the act is taken across the threshold, where it further shapes the suicide victim's experience.

Furthermore, the *intention* underlying suicide is of crucial importance. What is the reason for wanting to put an end to our life? Are we running away from a problem? Are we throwing our life away? Or do we think that we are sacrificing our life? Even this last purpose has its effects beyond the threshold.

Another decisive aspect is the suicide's *mental* state. Is the person suffering from a mental illness, or do they leave life with a clear mind? People suffering with a mental illness often continue to live out the terrible experiences they bore within them as a result of that illness, and they do not always realise that they have died. When they become aware that they have crossed the threshold, they often have difficulty recognising their life as their own. They cannot always tell what was truly theirs and what was the influence of the disease.

A middle-aged man who had committed suicide as a result of his mental illness reported a few days after his death how he had experienced the nature of his illness during his earthly life:

> The illness was always there, like a shadow, even in my parents' home. I didn't experience its onset as a sudden event, more like a presence that crept into my consciousness and took me over. I didn't notice how I disappeared into it; I thought the illness *was* me. I didn't have the inner resources to fight it because I had never experienced my own self before. Life was like a film in which you're playing a role, and then gradually over time you think you are this role . . . I've had delusions that had nothing to do with the world out there, they were the products of my own tortured, distorted inner world. The 'will to leave' [his intention to commit suicide] arose out of being demoralised, out of a feeling of hopelessness. I didn't know how else to get out of it.

He described the situation of suicide as follows:

> I fled from these delusions in a panic. It was like a fuse blew. I see the disease and I run away from it, but it's always with me. It tells me crazy things; I'm completely crazy from it. I don't even know what's happening to me; I don't understand anything any more. I have no anchor, no mind to hold me, just a whirlpool of nothing

89

sucking at me. I have run and run, uncoupled from the world. I've had fantasies of persecution; everything was like a nightmare in which I was caught alive.

However, the man shrank from his death. He did not want to look at it and wasn't sure if it had really taken place. Many images of his life were strange to him, as if they did not belong to him. He understood some of his past a little better, but there was much that surprised him. It seemed as if he were watching a film in which he only recognised individual sequences. The rest of his life was not familiar to him at all. After a lengthy conversation he answered the question of whether he could forgive himself: 'I still don't know what to forgive in all this. What was I?'

I asked the angels present what would happen to him now. They explained that he must first learn to relate to the life he had lived. Then he would be led to a place where he could find peace and healing. It is a spiritual 'recovery house', comparable to a sanatorium, where he would spend a long time surrounded by spiritual helpers. Just as severely ill people experience fever deliriums with oppressive fantasies, he would also be confronted repeatedly with his deed and with his life. The process that awaited him was not easy, but step by step he would find the connection to his own being again.

In addition to the emotional and mental aspects at the time of suicide, there is also the physical situation in which the person committing suicide finds themselves. For the members of our being, it makes a difference whether we forcibly tear ourselves out of a healthy physical body in the middle of life, or if we release ourselves from a body that is already in the process of dying. This should by no means be understood as an argument for euthanasia for old or seriously ill people. It should only lead to an awareness that for the different members of the human being, the way they detach themselves from earthly life makes a difference. Our inner being *always* experiences pain with this kind of death. It is only the quality of the pain that differs.

Seen from the spiritual side, suicide signifies an aborted life, a life not rounded off. The life painting is unfinished: its colour palette is not exhausted; its landscapes are not complete; it lacks certain nuances and brushstrokes. It is all the more our task to offer compassion, understanding and an inner light to a person who ends their life in this way. To condemn a suicide burdens their already difficult condition, but to give them forgiveness and confidence in their further path gives them back their dignity.

For those left behind, the death of a loved one by suicide can be a heavy burden to bear. Coming to terms with a suicide has a different quality and dimension to it than in the case of a natural death. For the families, aside from the grief and the pain of their loss, there are many unanswered questions, the biggest of all being 'why?' In many cases, the bereaved struggle with guilt and are plagued with doubts as to whether they could have done more to keep the departed from their deed.

After death the consciousness of the deceased who committed suicide remains close to the earth. They often circle around their relatives, wanting to explain themselves to them and to ask their forgiveness. For those left behind this has an incredibly stressful and leaden effect. They experience, albeit unknowingly, the loneliness, darkness, regret and despair that continuously emanate from the deceased. In the living, this can cause a strong longing for death and lead to depression or suicidal thoughts. In their soul's darkness, some suicides hang on to their relatives or friends because that is the only source of light they can see. To a considerable degree this weakens the relatives' and friends' own spiritual powers. Suicides who are not aware that they are dead can be a real danger for the bereaved. To put an end to their unbearable state they can try to carry out the suicide again through the possessed person. This significantly increases the potential for suicide in those 'possessed' in this way.

An extremely clear and conscious handling of suicides is therefore all the more important. We need to recognise the difference between our own pain and the pain of the suicide victim who may orbit us. Those left behind should also learn to distinguish – even more clearly than usual – between compassionately accompanying the dead and being 'possessed' by them. The intimate, selfless carrying of a friend in distress has an entirely different quality than spiritually and emotionally dragging along an uninvited guest. If we consider how high the worldwide number of suicides is, it becomes clear how large a number of living individuals are also affected by this matter.

Violent crimes and murders

After their death, it is not only people who have committed suicide who remain bound to their deeds. In the etheric world, murderers and felons, too, cannot at first detach themselves from the crimes they have committed: they are bound to the destructive forces of their crimes. During their life review, such deceased persons are confronted with the devastating consequences of their actions. This fills them with an appalling horror. They condemn themselves and do not consider themselves worthy of forgiveness.

In some cases, the victims of violence and murder also remain tied to the torture they have suffered, although this is by no means always the case. Whether a crime is experienced by the perpetrator or by the victim, in both cases it is a matter of profound shock. The affected person repeatedly experiences either the injustice they have perpetrated or the crime of which they were a victim.

The following example illustrates a case in which the person concerned, once he had passed over to the etheric world, found himself in the role of both perpetrator and victim.

A young man had taken the usual path of a petty criminal. Although he was characterised by a warmth of heart and a certain ecclesiastical religious character, his emotional instability meant he could not break out of the vicious cycle into which he had been drawn. He had begun with fraud and multiple thefts, followed by more serious crimes, after which he left the small town where he lived. Some of his victims, as well as the police, were looking for him. He went into hiding and tried several times to start over again, but each time failed. His list of crimes became longer and increasingly severe. He fled abroad, and his trail was lost for a long time.

Some years later I came across him as a deceased soul still bound to the earth. He was confined to a dark, narrow area of greyish mist in which strange figures continuously dragged him back and forth, never allowing him a moment's rest. He was tormented by terrible experiences and filled with the martyr's conviction that he was undeserving of forgiveness. The scene was strongly reminiscent of the places in which suicides are encountered, although some aspects were formed differently here. In the background, the deceased was aware of larger beings who stood guard and ensured that he could not escape his prison.

In conversation, I understood that the young man had been brutally murdered. His life had become increasingly entangled in dangerous criminal activities and he had been killed in revenge by other criminals. The experience of how his body was first maltreated and then destroyed was deeply traumatising. He remained trapped in these images and could not detach himself from them.

Moreover, he was tormented by his *own* crimes and the

grave injustices he had committed against other people. He suffered as victim and perpetrator; both identities tied him to horrible events in his life, which he experienced over and over again. He was neither able to forgive his tormentors nor was he able to forgive himself. He was sure that his punishment was to remain imprisoned in the dark realm in which he now found himself.

After a lengthy conversation, he was able to direct his attention to his angel. This helped to reassure him. When I provided him with further insights, he understood that he had *condemned himself* and had thereby tied himself to this state in which he believed he was bound for all eternity. He was now able to absorb the light that he suddenly perceived around him, and he was overwhelmed by the love and goodness of the beings that surrounded him.

It was then also possible for him to meet the being of Christ, who was shining in the background. It was profoundly moving to see how this young man, who had been in agony between worlds for years, sank to his knees and let the unconditional, eternal love of Christ flow into him. Now he was ready to forgive himself and his murderers, and together with his angel to leave this terrible place.

The path of a deceased soul who has suffered real agony over such a prolonged period does not lead from the etheric world directly into the soul world. Such souls are exhausted by their experience. Like those who have committed suicide, they must first undergo a degree of inner healing and discover new strength. Only then can they take on the further development that awaits them in the soul world. For this reason, they are also led to a place where the proper recuperation and healing can take place. This spiritual region is a kind of preliminary stage to the soul world and is subject to the direction of higher angelic beings.

Deceased persons from the higher soul and spirit worlds serve here and look after every newcomer.

The deceased souls requiring treatment spend different lengths of time here. Their inner state is recognisable by the amount of light in their surroundings: the gloomier and more disturbed their mood of soul, the darker and more constricted their space seems to be, whereas the more strongly they experience healing and the more strength they draw, the brighter their surroundings. The young man mentioned above spent several months at such a place of recovery. He underwent important inner processes, which then enabled him to take the actual step into the soul world. There he will confront his life in a new way.

Curses and black magic practices

The effect of curses is an area that is less well known in our current culture. We think that curses belong to ancient times, and they do indeed go back to the earliest civilisations. In the West we rarely meet this phenomenon in comparison to other parts of the world where curses or hexes belong more to folk tradition. But in working with the deceased, and above all in coming to terms with karmic blockages or problems of destiny, we do still encounter them.

Curses and imprecations are spiritual impulses that emanate from negative emotions with the intention of bringing disaster upon someone. Behind these impulses are emotions such as anger, hatred, selfishness, greed for power, envy, resentment, jealousy, a desire for revenge or feelings of powerlessness. Adversarial forces are always associated with spiritual energies generated in this way, which means that demonic beings of various types are at work here.

Curses can be pronounced casually or with conscious intent, meaning their effect can be diffused or more focused. The inner attitude of the victim also plays a crucial role here. If a person feels helpless and at the mercy of the curse, then these negative emotions can make them more vulnerable to attack. Likewise, if they react with indignation or anger, the negative energy gains strength and becomes even more powerful. However, if they anchor themselves in a true sense of their own self and know themselves to be untouchable in their spiritual core, they create a spiritual shield that protects them.

Beside curses and imprecations there are also black magic practices. These are employed with more targeted intentions and therefore have a far more destructive potential. Acts of black magic originate from conscious impulses of will that are of a wholly selfish character. Rudolf Steiner describes black magic as an egoism that leads to selfish spiritual acts: '[black magic] begins where occult activity is practised openly by those who are not in a position to expand their self-interests into world interests, who are unable to give greater importance to the interests of others.'[3] The practitioner of black magic has a knowledge of spiritual connections, but rather than placing this knowledge at the service of the world, they use it to advance their own purely personal interests.

Both curses and black magic activity can remain effective over prolonged periods. They create a variety of blockages and inhibit specific developmental processes, both in the incarnated and the excarnated state. On all levels of the afterlife, we meet deceased people who have not detached themselves from such entanglements. There are people who devoted themselves more or less consciously to dark practices during their lifetime and now remain possessed, or who attach themselves to other souls. There are those who long to free themselves from such powers, but don't know how; and those in contrast who consciously adhere to them and continue to work intentionally with these powers.

If we engage in redemptive work in former Nazi concentration camps or torture prisons in communist states, we find deceased persons who were and still are chained to black magic regimes. From prison guards to commanders, from so-called followers to prisoners who themselves had become perpetrators, we meet souls who have connected themselves to black magic in varying degrees of severity. At some point, each of these souls made a more or less deliberate decision to connect with evil. Such souls are neither free nor redeemed after the crossing of the threshold. The darkness of the powers to which they have committed themselves still overshadow and possess them.

Black magic bases itself in the Satanic element and wields its greatest influence where egoism and striving for power originate not from a vague emotional impulse, but from a deliberate decision. Our world today is strongly affected by this, even if our society is unaware of it. In certain structures of the economic, financial, and banking systems, in some areas of modern technology as well as in certain orders of political power, we encounter the workings of black magic influenced by such possessed deceased persons.

These deceased souls, more than all others, need the liberating help that can come to them from living people. But here it is not enough to send them forces of love and forgiveness, or to draw attention to the connection with the person's angel. The essence of such deceased persons must literally be cleansed of its black magic portions, like the excising of diseased tissue from the physical body. This purification work is done with the assistance of spiritual helpers from the higher spiritual worlds who work through the 'I' and have undergone special preparation for this work.

Looking at the earth's entire etheric aura, we can conclude that the progress of human beings through the afterlife has fallen into considerable disorder. There are, of course, deceased persons who have detached themselves from the earth in a light-filled way and are continuing their onward journey with an open heart. It is a joy to accompany these souls and witness their ascent into higher spheres. But what was hitherto accepted as the regular course of development for a person after death is no longer the case: there are just too many souls who go through this process in an unhealthy and discordant way. Working with the dead clearly shows that a considerable portion of humanity remains bound to the earth on the etheric level, which places a corresponding burden on the earth's aura. Etheric spaces that should animate and strengthen the planet are congested and overpopulated by souls in need of help. This fact calls upon us to take responsibility for these areas, which have a direct effect on our earthly spaces. It is therefore encouraging to see that even a small spark of consciousness, when coupled with active support, can bring about concrete change.

8

When Children Die

It is not about letting the child go;
what mother, what father could let go of their beloved child?
It is about finding out what this child's message was to you,
how it changed you, how much love has grown in you,
what therefore did your child 'draw out of you in love'?
How much new love has grown in you?
Your searching will help you to pick up your child's
imprint and carry it further.

Anselm Grün

Losing a child is the greatest pain a person can suffer. Unlike the loss of our parents, close friends, or even our life partner, our entire being is put to the test in a way never before imagined. From a spiritual point of view, it is also a unique situation when children die, but in contrast to the pain and despair felt by the grieving family, in the spiritual world the souls of children are received with an exceptional amount of light and love. Angelic beings and those deceased people familiar to the child receive them and take care of them in a joyful atmosphere. Children often experience crossing the threshold in a playful manner and quite naturally blend into this new dimension of being.

The development of children after death is subject to different laws and rhythms than is that of adults for the simple reason that children tend to be burdened with far fewer emotional entanglements. The 'baggage' of being human that adults carry across the threshold is hardly present in children. The moral and ethical experiences of a twelve-year-old child are only a preliminary testing of what it is to be human, and so from a spiritual point of view they are not held fully accountable for their actions. For these reasons, their passage through the etheric and soul worlds is structured differently. They are guided from one stage of development to the next by angelic beings who are dedicated to this task. Deceased people from higher spheres who have selflessly given themselves to this service are also active here.

After crossing the threshold, children can still participate in family life on earth owing to the ease with which they can move between worlds.

Talking to a mother and her three children, who had all died in a car accident, I was able to see how the children flew to their father. He was the only one to survive the accident and was seriously injured in hospital. In the spiritual world you do not have to 'fly' anywhere, you need only think of a place and you are there, but for the children it was like a game to fly to earth.

'In the morning we go sledding down to Dad on sunbeams. We surround him and sometimes tickle him and take it in turns to sit astride him,' they said, giggling. 'He doesn't notice it, but his angel lets us do it. His angel is always there, watching over him, and he smiles at us. The elemental being connected to Daddy's body looks forward to our arrival too. He says that we bring him powers of light with which he can work to help heal Daddy's body and soul.'

When I asked them why they had to die so young, they explained that they only needed to 'touch the earth like a drop', nothing more. 'There were a number of scenarios prepared in advance of our birth. The plan was so firm that if it had not happened in this way [through the car crash], then another situation would have arisen that would have made it possible for us to leave. We all agreed to do this long before we were born.'

A few weeks later I looked in again on this family and found their situation had changed somewhat. 'I am with the children less and less now,' the mother explained to me. 'They have moved on in their development and going forward our paths are quite different. The children don't just play as they did in the beginning; the angels have taken them to begin a higher spiritual schooling. They can still be with their father at lightning speed, but otherwise they have become more detached from the earth. Their attention is directed towards the community of spiritual beings with whom they now live.'

Many families have the impression that their deceased child is still with them, and this feeling is correct. But this does not mean that these deceased children have remained trapped in the etheric world. Children continue to accompany their families and experience what happens in the souls of their parents and siblings. It is also easier for them to make themselves noticeable in their relatives' dreams than it would be for a deceased adult. When children experience their family's pain and sadness, they give comfort, light, confidence, and love. It is also essential for the further development of deceased children that the bereaved learn to let go of them in good time. This frees them up and they do not experience their earthly family as a task that requires their constant attention.

A young woman was pregnant with twins, a boy and a girl. The girl died during pregnancy and the boy was born a few months later. Every night, and only at night, when the mother nursed the boy, she had the impression that she was holding a girl in her arms. Again and again, she had to remind herself that she had given birth to a boy. When observed spiritually, it could be seen that the deceased girl came to her mother every night. She loved the silence of those hours and the atmosphere that surrounded mother and child. The girl would lay her head on her mother's breast and this gave the mother the impression that she was nursing a girl instead of a boy. In conversation with this girl's spirit, it became clear that her brief contact with the earth had been planned from the beginning. It had not been her intention to incarnate and live an earthly life at that time. But she still had certain experiences from her previous life to catch up with, which she could now do through the close bond she had with this person who was her mother. After two months the girl no longer came in this form. She hovered around the family for another two years, but from a greater distance and with a more inwardly liberated mood of soul.

In my conversations with deceased children, I was told that their death had already been planned in the time before birth. This also applies to unborn children who stop their incarnation during pregnancy. They all have a specific task to fulfil or lesson to learn in the earthly world. For the families, the pain of losing a child can awaken deeper insight into the spiritual side of existence: questions about the meaning of life take on a greater profundity, and issues of love and faith and letting go are experienced in completely new ways.

A young woman lost her seriously ill first-born son a few days after the birth. Grieving and in pain, she visited a group for 'orphaned parents'. There she met people who told her about anthroposophic therapies and Waldorf education. Although this was all new to her and a little bit strange, it nevertheless spoke to something deep within her. With the help of a eurythmy therapist and an art therapist, she was able to work through her loss and restore her emotional balance. She found the courage and the confidence to become pregnant again, and this time the birth took place without complications. The second child was born in perfect health. The mother later decided to send the child to a Waldorf kindergarten and also began to take spiritual ideas more seriously.

The first, deceased child had remained in the vicinity of this family. The boy's spirit provided the impulse for the mother to visit the group, and it was he who gave her the confidence to become pregnant again. The boy's spirit also gave her the inspiration to send his sibling to the Waldorf kindergarten. When all of this had happened, he felt that his task with this family had been fulfilled and he withdrew into the spiritual world to continue along his path.

In this sense the destiny of deceased children is fulfilled precisely during this, albeit short, time. Hardly any child dies 'before their time', no matter how unspeakably tragic their death is for their family. There are exceptions, however, most notably in the case of violent crimes and wars where destructive powers intervene in the destiny of a soul. Yet even in these cases, it is astonishing to see that many of these events were planned for before birth – if only as *potential* destinies.

Irrespective of the circumstances of death, it is clear that when children die many spiritual beings are on hand to offer assistance, more so than is the case with adults. Children still experience themselves as spiritual beings: their hearts are pure and completely open, they are not held back by fear nor have they become hardened by fixed ideas and rigid dogmas like many adults. It hardly ever happens that children get trapped in the etheric world because of traumatic experiences.

For children who are aborted during pregnancy, it is important that their mother or parents internally adopt them. For the mother, the situation of an abortion is usually associated with feelings of strain, insecurity, discord and self-reproach. It is a tremendous psychological burden, especially for the mother. This makes it even more important to deal with the situation consciously.

For this, it is essential to know that the soul of each child feels a deep and intimate love for the being of their mother, and because of this love the child is able to show understanding and respect for the mother's decision, however it has come about. The child may be disappointed that it cannot grasp this opportunity for incarnation, but it has confidence that another opportunity will present itself at a later time.

Since the child perceives what lives in the soul of the mother, it is even more important that she does not hold onto feelings of guilt or remorse, or that she withdraws into her pain. Nor is suppressing feelings a helpful solution here, because all suppressed emotion continues to have an effect, even if unconsciously. Instead, it is helpful if the mother enters into an inner dialogue with the child's soul. For this, she does not need to be able to perceive the child's spirit. It is enough for her to have an intimate heart conversation with the child in which she explains her view of the existing circumstances to them. She can express her regret and grief and ask the child for forgiveness.

At the same time, she can trust that the child will accept her approach with sympathy and understanding.

A small ritual – perhaps with a prayer, a candle, flower or with a symbol – can create a dignified atmosphere for such a dialogue and can also serve as a farewell between the mother and the child's soul. The child feels seen and recognised, and the mother no longer need feel at the mercy of her inner conflict. In this way, the situation is clearly addressed. The child can now bring closure to the experience and move on to new experiences. Some children will have the courage to try a new incarnation with the same mother, or incarnate in entirely different families, whereas others return to the earth sphere only much later.

9

A Second Death

Take what thou wilt; I leave it thee.
It comes from thee; let it be thine again.
I no longer need to lean on thee
There where I shall now find myself at home.

Christian Morgenstern, 'We Have Found a Path'

The time in the etheric world, with all its associated experiences, forms the first stage in the human being's development after death. As the carrier of our memories and habits, the etheric body completes its task for this current incarnation with the illumination of the life review: that great event in which the life just ended is viewed by the deceased person in a purely objective manner. With this, the etheric body has fulfilled its mission, and just as the physical body is set aside when a person reaches the end of their earthly life and no longer needs it, so now the etheric body is cast off. After their physical death on earth, the human being undergoes another death in the spiritual world: this is their etheric death.

During a traditional Christian funeral, the following lines are read out: 'Earth to earth, ashes to ashes, dust to dust'. This reminds us that through death the substances that formed our physical body from the earth are now returned to the earth. This is also the case with the etheric body, which now dissolves and returns its substance to the wider etheric world. This usually takes place around three days after crossing the threshold, but can take between several days and several weeks. If the deceased stays trapped in the etheric world, the time is longer.

Free of their etheric body, the deceased person experiences vast new spaces opening up to their vision: this is the soul world. One deceased young woman describes this step as follows:

> I am still standing at the border of these two worlds,
> but I perceive this new world opening up to me more
> and more. It calls to me and I know the path I must take
> leads that way. My angel is with me, waiting patiently.
> He gives me to understand that the path is now open for
> me. I can go on myself, and that fills me with happiness.

The deceased person experiences their etheric death as an ever-widening extension of their being into the world ether: their entire etheric body breathes itself out into this infinite expanse. Everything that up until now has formed their memory begins to dissolve and the deceased person loses awareness of their everyday self. Only an extract remains from their etheric body to be carried over into the next incarnation. For the deceased person, this is a powerful and emancipating experience.

If we accompany such an event inwardly, we see the deceased person spreading out above the terrestrial sphere, becoming ever larger. We experience, too, an ever-increasing expansion of our being. At first, this creates a strange and frightening feeling: we feel that our being could continue to expand indefinitely before disappearing completely into thin air. We want to contract again to maintain our consciousness. But if we overcome this initial fear and allow the experience to unfold, we perceive that the space into which we expand is not empty but completely interwoven with life. It is the living, vibrating, light-filled etheric world that weaves through and enlivens the entire space surrounding the earth.

During this event, the memories and experiences stored in the deceased person's etheric body pass over into the world ether. The etheric world is changed by what the deceased brings to it from their life on earth. It acquires a slightly different colouration and imprint, and new experiences are inscribed into the ether that help to form what Rudolf Steiner and others called the Akashic Chronicle: the great cosmic script which is a record of everything that takes place on earth. Through all of our existence and activity we are helping to shape future worlds which, like the earth organism, are in a constant process of change and development.

During their etheric death, the human being's higher spiritual bodies, their soul body and their I, free themselves from the expanding etheric body. The deceased person now awakens to a higher consciousness and experiences themselves as a being in the soul realm. In meditation, we can meet the deceased in this phase in symbolic images that show them being 'newly dressed': angels weave coloured garments of light around the person who has arrived in the soul world. Since symbols are archetypal signs for spiritual connections, it is easy to understand these images as depicting the taking on of a soul mantle after the etheric sheath has been discarded.

On one occasion I saw a deceased friend of mine surrounded by several angels. Her posture was upright and at the same time very mobile. Her eyes shone as they did when she was at her most beautiful on earth, and she was filled with a great, luminous joy. Her time in the etheric world had not been easy.

I asked her what had happened and she showed me how she had removed the grey veils of experience that had previously surrounded her. The angels who had received her in this new sphere, were now weaving beautiful garments of golden light around her. Her figure merged with these coloured veils and in this radiant garment she was able to enter the soul world.

Just as dying in the earthly world leads to a resurrection in the etheric, so also is the etheric death a resurrection in the soul world. For the deceased, their time in the soul world opens up new dimensions of consciousness and being, which allow them to deepen and enrich their entire soul life.

10

The Encounter with the Being of Christ

Always behind the wall
of your destiny
Christ stands – and waits.

Fred Poeppig, *Steps on the Way*

In the etheric sphere the deceased person encountered for the first time the totality of their biography, presented to them in the form of an objective life review that revealed their life's essence. To some extent the person also experienced the impact their actions had on other people and their environment. The task that lies ahead of them now as they enter the soul world, is to experience the effects of their earthly life as concretely as possible, and from this form the impulses necessary for a future life on earth.

To prepare for this, the deceased person has a significant encounter, one that every human being has in the life after death: an encounter with the being of Christ. Since his death on Golgotha, Christ has accompanied the development of humankind on earth. Turning towards him means striving towards our highest divine ideal. During a person's life on earth they can cultivate a deep inner connection to Christ, which can lead to a direct experience of Christ's loving presence among us. In the life after death, too, human beings can turn to Christ at any time, who then appears as a shining spirit figure. Their own searching for Christ is decisive in this encounter, and whether they choose to search for him or not is left to them as an entirely free decision. Such experiences within earthly life are therefore rare.

But there is one point at which human beings, regardless of their religious or ideological convictions, come face to face with the being of Christ: this is at the transition from the etheric world to the soul world. Here, Christ receives every human soul on their journey through the life after death. This encounter, which affects the whole human being, is one of the most meaningful for their development after death.

The deceased person has discarded their etheric body and their consciousness has awakened in a soul-spiritual environment full of living colours and moving forms. Everything that surrounds them here is ensouled living substance that weaves an existence of sounds, rich colours and manifold harmonious shapes. The figure of Christ awaits them in a clear, light-filled landscape. The human soul perceives the sublime, all-encompassing light and love of Christ that now floods their whole being. They have a truly profound sense of being seen and understood and they feel the deepest reverence for Christ. In its openness and honesty, this is an overwhelming experience.

For a second time human souls, now in the company of Christ, review their past earthly life. Here there is no film-like projection of scenes from their life as there was in the etheric sphere. Instead, the essence of their being, what came to expression in their mortal life, stands before them like a piece of sculpture or some other completed work of art. In Christ's presence, the human being is filled to a far greater extent with compassion and insight. What was merely touched upon in the etheric review of their life is here experienced more intensely and with a greater clarity. The joy we have felt is magnified, our pain is sharper, feelings of guilt and shame weigh more heavily on us, and the compassion we have shown towards others is deepened and made stronger. Through the encounter with Christ, the deceased person acquires a fundamentally new understanding of their own nature.

A twenty-seven-year-old woman, who died in a car accident, described the beginning of her time in the soul world:

> It is a living world of dancing, flowing, weaving colours that you cannot imagine on earth. I live in all the colours of the sky. Everything here is life and colour; everything is living light. I have met Christ. I have looked at my life with him. So much was laid out in my life – in ordinary, everyday events – that was hidden from me beneath the threshold of my everyday consciousness. Christ allowed me to recognise this and to understand myself and my destiny anew. I did not know how much a human life can mean: how much wisdom and how many precious things are tucked into it by the forces of destiny. All of this is connected with the development of our being over thousands of years. The arc of our incarnations is immense!

> Christ looked into my eyes and there was such mildness and infinite love in his gaze. It was sublime. He is a brother to us all, a brother full of understanding and

compassion, but with a different view of our being. Fatherly wisdom shines from his head, healing love flows from his heart, and from his eyes there speaks the Source of All Love! All my sorrow and pain has passed away; my whole being has been purified by the healing strength that flows through me from him. I feel as if I have been reborn, as if I have been created anew, even though I have existed for such a long time. I am free of all the cares I carried around with me in earthly life, and with a loving will I can now prepare myself for a new life. I have become one with heaven and with my destiny.

As the second person of the Trinity, Christ is the Son of God, but through his incarnation in Jesus of Nazareth, he became human and experienced all that human beings undergo during their life on earth. He was himself subject to temptations, pain and grief. He knows hesitation, indecision, inner struggle, doubt and despair. He is therefore not only the divine Son but also our brother and friend, accompanying us on the long path of our development.

Not everyone can bear Christ's all-knowing gaze. Some feel unworthy in the face of this encounter with supreme divinity and condemn themselves. The effects of their double, or doppelgänger, still resound here in feelings of powerlessness, fear, anger, hatred, shame and remorse. They are unable to forgive themselves or others and remain at odds with life. Even when Christ explains to them that they can free themselves from these shadows whenever they want, not everyone can. They draw these unresolved issues along with them through the spiritual world and into their next incarnation.

Christ, however, does not judge human beings, but instead

asks them questions about the decisive events in their life. In this way, he opens the person's eyes to how they have created their own life and how it has consequently shaped the world. Understanding what was self-created gives rise to the knowledge of what a person needs to do in order to develop their being in the future, and this creates a powerful stimulus for the formation of a new life on earth, a new incarnation.

The focus therefore is on the consequences of the life just lived. We not only experience our destiny as interwoven with the entire fate of the earth but also in what manner: how it embellishes or disfigures the shape of the world. We realise that our destiny or karma is at the same time the earth's karma: through all our existence and activity we bear responsibility for the future of the world. This goes far beyond what is otherwise meant by an encounter with our own self and knowledge of our destiny. Rudolf Steiner describes this encounter with Christ in the soul world as a moment of true enlightenment for human beings.[4]

As deep an impression that the meeting with Christ may create, it does not mean the human soul has been purified and healed. The actual work of healing and redemption still lies ahead of human beings in the soul world. The encounter with Christ is a preparation for this work.

11

Time in the Lower Soul World

Seek in your own being
And you will find the world;
Seek in the world wide being
And you will find yourself

Rudolf Steiner, *Truth Wrought Words*

In the soul world, thoughts and feelings and impulses of will form an outer world of weaving light and colour. Everything is lively and dynamic, and yet at the same time wisely ordered. In this world, which it is difficult for our purely earthbound imaginations to grasp, the deceased person rises to ever higher levels of consciousness in their ongoing spiritual evolution. As always, they are accompanied by various angelic beings.

Having already experienced their biography twice, and in different ways, the deceased person now experiences it for a third time, again from a new perspective. Everything the person did to others during their life on earth they now feel as though these things had been done to them: all the joy they brought, all the suffering they caused, they experience as their own. What a person created outwardly on earth now becomes their inner world, and what they experienced as their inner world on earth – every thought, feeling and wish – forms their outer world in the world of soul. They stand amid the repercussions of their entire soul life, recognising the effects that their thoughts and deeds had upon their fellow creatures and upon the world.

During our incarnation, any bad thoughts we have towards a person weakens that person's life force, unpleasant feelings have a damaging effect on their aura, hurtful deeds have an impact on their will impulses. Conversely, we can say that good thoughts about another strengthen the other, sincere and heartfelt feelings makes the other's aura shine, and helpful actions support them in fulfilling their destiny. In the incarnated state these realities do not penetrate our daily awareness, but every night during sleep we live in these effects along with all other people, even though we may not be aware of it.

Time spent in the lower soul world is therefore a revival of these nightly experiences, which the deceased person now lives through in reverse order. According to Rudolf Steiner this takes on average about one-third the length of a person's earthly life, which is approximately how long a person spends asleep during the course of their life. This is just a general rule, however, and can vary from person to person. If, for example, the deceased person felt envy towards a person during their lifetime, in the astral sphere they now live entirely in the hurtful, stabbing atmosphere of that envy. They are exposed to the feeling of weakening or strengthening, of prevention or encouragement that they have bestowed upon others. The loving, kind, positive successes in the biography envelop them here in glowing, joyful images and give them a spiritual experience of bliss and of communion with other spiritual beings. The loveless, negative, distorted, selfish or destructive actions and thoughts surround them as an atmosphere of deprivation and torment and lead to an experience of loneliness and pain.

Experiencing our life in all its effects produces in us a desire to create a balance. This develops into a strong impulse that draws us back into earthly life, where we strive to make up for our previous misdeeds, balance out our one-sided tendencies, and fill in the missing elements of our soul's biography. These individual experiences lay concrete foundations for our next life on earth, and these will be worked on at later stages together with higher spiritual beings.

Human beings in the soul world appear differently to spiritual perception than those who are still in the etheric world. While a strong correspondence remains in the etheric world between a deceased person and how they formerly appeared on earth, in the soul world their outer spiritual form is less sharply (or perhaps that should be less rigidly) defined: it is more permeable. The person appears younger and parts of their form seem to consist of moving veils of light. At the same time, their essence is more strongly perceptible. If we move inwardly towards a person in the soul world, we often find them occupied with a single sequence from their former life. This provides information about the events they are currently experiencing and which phase they are working through in their life. Since the confrontation with our soul's biography takes place in reverse order, the deceased person appears in an ever younger form.

In general, human beings in the soul world feel much further away from the earth. Their consciousness is no longer focused on the earthly, but to a much greater extent on their experiences in the soul world. If they have a specific concern, for example if they want to communicate something to a bereaved person, they can concentrate their energy and appear spiritually to them. The ability to move between worlds is still a given, but it demands an effort from them. Usually, the living person has a feeling or a thought that reminds them of the deceased, but normally they do not consciously notice that the deceased person is in fact present.

In the soul world, a deceased person still experiences the emotions of the bereaved: prayers, good thoughts and loving memories fill them with warmth and illuminate their world of experience; mourning, bitterness or resentment are stressful and aggravating. It is therefore helpful if the relatives and friends concerned develop a feeling for whether the person needs help in processing their life.

Coming to terms with the effects of their soul life requires the deceased person to acknowledge everything that has to do with their nature. This can be harrowing work. In many biographies there are experiences that are difficult to cope with. The encounter with the being of Christ that has already taken place has enabled a clear understanding of our earthly biography and has given us impulses for the future. But despite this, carrying out the necessary soul work is often only partially successful. Many human beings in this soul world encounter aspects of their personality that they do not like and cannot accept. They find it difficult to integrate what has been repressed, such as feelings of guilt or other traumatising emotions that are locked away in the unconscious. Whatever a person cannot accept as belonging to them is not penetrated with the light of consciousness. It remains unredeemed, unprocessed. It forms something like a weight in the soul, which the deceased does not want to acknowledge, but which is nevertheless connected to them.

Even if the deceased is trying to face up to themselves and is always in contact with their angel, it can happen that they do not quite succeed in shining a light into all the hidden corners of their personality. The prerequisite for grasping and changing something is first to recognise it sincerely. Accordingly, work on our biography, both during earthly life and in the soul world, needs to be carried out as consciously as possible. Here the bereaved can help by accompanying the deceased in thought and by bringing those areas closer to them that were parts of their shadow, their doppelgänger. It is essential to do this as objectively as possible, without reproach or condemnation. In this way, we can remain in open and friendly partnership with the deceased during their life review. We can make our own insights available to them, encouraging them and expressing confidence that they will find the strength to accept these difficult experiences.

Beautifying or ignoring problematic topics, which dependants tend to do after a person's death, are of no help to the deceased person. On the contrary, this behaviour strengthens their denial and distorts their gaze. Nor do accusations, reproaches, rejection, or anger directed at them help. This makes it more difficult for the deceased to deal with the relevant subject area. It is essential to have an honest view that reflects the deceased's personality lovingly and at the same time clearly and objectively.

12

Effects of Unredeemed Portions of the Soul

It is not those events which hurry by,
Making division of your soul into
Both joy and strife,
Not these your life's true core. Elusively
It moves beyond your sense's goal
Between the lines of life.

Manfred Kyber, *Genius Astri*

In order to progress in our development, recognition and action are necessary. As has already been mentioned, the human being's encounter with Christ at the threshold to the soul world and with the totality of their soul life is a moment of profound awakening involving the highest degree of consciousness. This corresponds to the step of recognition. However, the next step – action – depends on how open we are to this experience and on our willingness to deal with what has been recognised. Success in taking the first step does not imply success in the second. The encounter with Christ does not relieve us of the necessary soul-work we must do; instead it gives us the impetus to carry it out. Whether or not we are successful in this depends entirely on the extent to which we take up this impetus and implement it.

If, for example, a deceased person is unwilling to confront certain aspects of their personality or acknowledge the harmful effects their actions have had, then they are unable to work on this part of themselves. This unacknowledged, unredeemed part of their soul remains split off from their consciousness. It descends with them into their next life on earth, their next incarnation, leading to renewed, deep-seated difficulties of an entirely unconscious character. It makes an enormous difference, therefore, whether we resolve to bring about a change in the next incarnation, or whether we leave an issue untreated. In the first case, even if the problem is not present in our day-consciousness, transformation is still possible since our higher 'I' will have ordered the events of our life in order to bring about this opportunity. In the second case, because the impetus for it is not present, there is less possibility of change: we are exposed to the forces of the destiny of our past and risk becoming even more entangled in it.

In therapy a middle-aged woman reported that for her whole life she had felt herself to be an outsider and a victim. As a dreamy child, she found it difficult to find her way in this world and felt quite estranged. At school, she was a good girl and tried hard, but she had great difficulties meeting intellectual demands and social conditions. She had no friends and was often teased; her classmates did not accept her. Adolescence was an especially confusing time for her and she struggled to understand the changes in her classmates: the formation of cliques, the flirting, and the interest in the opposite sex. All of this overwhelmed her; she even found it repulsive. At the same time, however, she envied those to whom she did not belong. She experienced her whole existence as laborious and herself as a misunderstood victim of undeserved loneliness. Other people were strange and inaccessible to her.

After completing her education, she married and had children. This had been her life's dearest dream. At last, she felt that things were working out for her. However, her happiness did not last. The role of mother overtaxed her; she now felt continuously annoyed by her children, insufficiently supported by her husband, and abandoned by the world around her. She became dissatisfied and depressed, unable to find balance in her life. After a few years, her husband left her. He could no longer bear her constant dissatisfaction and turned to another woman. Once again, the client felt confirmed in the role of victim. From her perspective, she was the one who had sacrificed everything for the family; her husband, on the other hand, was the ungrateful one who had abandoned her and the children. She was unwilling to acknowledge that she herself had played a significant and active part in these events.

A retrospective showed her in a past life as a grouchy, grumpy, ill-tempered man who regularly abused and insulted the people around him. He accused everyone of evil intentions, but always felt himself in the right. In the afterlife, his soul was unwilling to accept these negative traits as belonging to it. It therefore entered its next incarnation, this time as a woman, with these unacknowledged issues and was required to encounter them again. The classmates in the woman's present life were the people she had formerly insulted and who now instinctively disliked and rejected her. The social exclusion that she experienced was the effect of her earlier social actions, and the feeling she had of being estranged from the world was a consequence of her lack of love for other people in her past life. Despite intensive therapeutic work, this woman only managed to a small extent to accept her experience as belonging to her or to recognise the difficulties of her destiny as opportunities for growth.

This case shows, in a very condensed form, that repression and unconsciousness during the soul review of life can lead to a lack of understanding of our later destiny. In certain contexts, such persons feel themselves to be victims because they were not conscious enough in the years before their birth to create this life. Unexamined, hurtful social behaviour in one life leads to social alienation in the next, as we have seen. The unseen parts of a personality from the previous life are carried along by the person's doppelgänger and they remain trapped in the same complex of issues. It can be difficult to find a solution since there is no access to the origin of the problem.

Acknowledging and working with these repressed traits, however, shines a light into these shadowy parts of the soul and ultimately wrests power over these issues from the doppelgänger. At the beginning of the next incarnation, the relevant problems are indeed not yet dealt with; but through the work carried out consciously in the soul world and the resolutions that were formed as a result, the soul creates scenarios and possibilities for dealing with them.

If a person does not carry out this work willingly and independently, the angelic beings who help to shape destiny give the soul a chance to gain access to its repressed motives. These are called 'sensitisation incarnations' in which repeatedly difficult or painful experiences draw our attention to just those issues with which we have not dealt. The suffering undergone here must not be thought of as a punishment, but as a chance to recognise and resolve the deeper problems connected to our life.

Of course, dealing with what lives in the soul not only affects the person's future. Associating with such a deceased person in the soul world can also have an effect on those they've left behind. Suppressed soul aspects can burden or possess incarnated (living) individuals in the form of attachments if there is a resonance between them.

Deceased persons who are trapped in the soul world have a different effect on incarnated individuals than do the dead who are trapped in the etheric world. They do not appear immediately to the spiritual eye as a visible figure, but their presence is noticeable and detectable. They work in a person's aura, and while their influence seems subtler at first than that of the deceased in the etheric, nevertheless it can be powerful and decisive.

The sense of obligation and unresolved ties

Someone who has suffered a sudden death has had little opportunity to free themselves from their human ties or their sense of obligation to their surviving dependants. Their attention can remain at least partially bound to them. The sadness and concern of a mother for her small children, her responsibility towards her lonely spouse or her parents who need care, can lead the deceased mother to circle them continually with a part of her soul. The deceased's constant concern can have an aggravating effect on the bereaved, however, because it expresses both an overestimation of her ability to act and a lack of trust in the wise guidance of destiny.

A man died at the age of sixty-eight. He was a controlling and forceful person. In the last years of his life his focus was mainly on his only grandson, who grew up without a father and who, in contrast to the grandfather, had a gentle, dreamy nature. The grandfather despised the tender approach his wife and the boy's mother took in raising him; he believed his grandson should be educated to be a 'real man'. After his death, the grandfather felt obligated to instil in his grandson this distorted ideal of masculinity and he took possession of the boy with the dominant part of his soul. Over time, seemingly inexplicable changes occurred in the boy's nature: fits of rage alternated with apathy, and his behaviour became increasingly unpredictable.

In therapeutic work, the mother recognised the effect of the deceased grandfather on the boy and was able to dissolve this possession.

In this and similar cases it is a matter of insufficiently dissolved bonds or emotional dependence. These can have their origin in both a sense of obligation and in unprocessed feelings of jealousy or possessiveness.

Addictions and compulsions

Addictions and compulsions, which are the most pronounced types of dependencies, have powerful effects after death. Substance addictions, such as alcohol and drug addictions, as well as those not involving substances, such as compulsive gambling and addictions to sex, computers, or work, originate from deep-seated and unresolved psychological issues. The problem of dependency therefore relates to the unacknowledged part of the human being's soul life and results in severe consequences in the soul world. After death, the physical body can no longer serve as an instrument for the satisfaction of addiction, but the emotional and mental dependency remains. It quite often happens that a deceased person seeks to satisfy their still-existing cravings by occupying living people. They cling to a person's aura, nourishing that person's dependency and intensifying their addictive behaviour. Or they are drawn to places that resonate with their cravings, such as drug-trafficking areas, pubs, brothels and amusement arcades. These sites possess an energy field that has a perceptibly depressing or draining effect.

Distorted self-image and repressed personality traits

Other difficulties we face in our encounter with ourselves arise from a distorted self-image. This can come about either through self-aggrandisement or self-negation. Self-aggrandisement is based on feelings of inferiority: we feel small when faced with the world and at the same time feel inadequate or dissatisfied with ourselves. Such people compensate for this experience through ego inflation, by imagining themselves to be more than they are. We also encounter a weak self-image in cases of self-negation, but one that works to undermine our potential and sell ourselves short. Both types, however, are based on a lack of self-love and low self-esteem. People suffering from such distortions find it difficult to establish a healthy relationship to themselves in the soul world and to integrate those parts of their soul life that were hidden from them during their lifetime. They are afraid to take responsibility for what they cannot see in themselves.

Character and personality traits that do not fit our idea of who we are can also cause us serious problems. By this we mean dissociated parts of our soul life, such as suppressed sexual desire, power struggles, and feelings of envy and hatred. If we cannot accept the reality of who we are as it is revealed to us in the soul world, if the discrepancy between this and our cherished self-image is too great, then those aspects which we deny in ourselves can assume an independent life of their own. They continue to search for a field of action and can attach themselves to people with similar traits or related issues.

One man who was regarded by many as an honourable family man, and who felt himself to be morally decent, had for decades regularly visited brothels. During his life review he was faced with the dilemma of having to confront these repressed and contradictory aspects of his personality. Since he was in self-denial about his actions, he could not bear to accept them and affirm this discrepancy in his character. The split-off parts of his soul life then fastened onto his son, who had sexual problems of his own. Sometime after his father's death, the son grew restless and felt an incessant urge to obtain sexual satisfaction via chat rooms and similar online portals. He spent a lot of money on them, which led to him going into debt and putting his marriage at risk.

It should be stated here that dubious activities by living people cannot simply be blamed on the deceased. Possession by a deceased person, or by split-off parts of their soul life, only takes place when a similar, or at least analogous, emotional resonance exists within a living person. However, it is essential to know that such possession by the deceased can exacerbate already existing problems in a person's life and lead to serious behavioural changes.

Fear, ideologies and fanaticism

Fear presents a fundamental obstacle in a human being's emotional development. It also has an aggravating effect in the soul world, where it can numb the soul's powers of self-reflection and hinder further progress. Rigid ideologies and dogmatic ways of thinking also have an obstructing effect.

Fanaticism, which springs from these sources and is always paired with hatred, often triggers possessions, such as in nationalist and terrorist groups and other extremist movements. The deceased fanatic finds in living followers a field of action for the unilluminated parts of their soul life. They cling to the follower's aura and act through it.

Severe trauma

As has already been discussed, shocks and traumas leave deep psychological traces. Even after death, both victims and perpetrators of violent acts are often unable to cope with what they have undergone. For many, although by no means all, these experiences were so traumatising that they cannot be integrated, either on the etheric or on the soul level. In many cases, those parts of a person's soul connected with these unprocessed experiences remain at the scene of the event or crime and affect the spiritual energies there.

Multiple possessions

When a possessed person dies, it usually happens that they still do not see through their possession in the life after death. They cannot reclaim the affected area of their being and restore the integrity of their selfhood. They continue to act according to the possessed part of their soul life and in turn occupy another living person. This then leads to multiple possessions. This needs to be recognised in the work of redemption and then removed layer by layer.

Mental illnesses

Multiple possessions are also associated with mental illnesses. Possession by deceased persons is, *as a rule*, the case with schizophrenia and delusional disorders, as well as with dissociative personality disorders. In psychoses, obsessive-compulsive disorders, paranoia and schizoid personality disorders, possession *may* be present. It may also be present in some phobias and severe forms of depression.

If a person dies whose experience was not centred in a healthy life of soul, then their time in the soul world is extremely difficult. Their relationship to themselves is shattered by the mental illness or by the possession. Their inner and outer worlds were not in balance during their life on earth and they were not able to perform many of their actions out of their own being. They have already experienced the confusion of this in the etheric review of their life. Now, during the soul review of their life, their confusion deepens as they confront the reality of their soul life. Their inner world, which comes towards them from the outside, is incomprehensible to them; they cannot identify with many events of their life and cannot integrate them.

In such a confused state, a deceased person usually seeks a connection to the familiar world of those they left behind or the institution in which they lived. They look for support and help from them, but in their disturbed condition they can quickly become a burden or threat to those persons with whom they connect.

Suicides

Those who commit suicide are both victims and perpetrators of their actions. Not only on the etheric level but also in the soul world they usually have great difficulties in enduring the effects of their actions and forgiving themselves. They realise that through suicide they have turned away from the spiritual world and disregarded the principles of creation. They have forfeited the fulfilment of their destiny this time around. Their darkened inner world now surrounds them in gloomy, frightening images. They experience the deep pain of the bereaved. This fills them with grief and regret and draws them back to their relatives. The condition of such a soul can lie like a grey, oppressive cloud over the family, resulting in fatigue, anxiety, depression or suicidal thoughts among the relatives.

A thirty-two-year-old drug addict committed suicide. He left behind a young wife and two small children. For a long time he remained trapped in the etheric world. He was in a desperate state, constantly circling both the family and the drug milieu that had so strongly influenced him. The children repeatedly complained about nightmares. His wife, who often felt him with her, accompanied him with earnest prayers. She tirelessly brought him understanding, love and compassion, and as time passed, he slowly managed to move away from the earth. But his destructive actions towards his family followed him into the soul world. His wife did not experience him as distinctly as before, but she felt continuously exhausted and depressed. When one of the children suddenly had a seizure, she realised she could no longer cope with this burden alone and sought therapeutic help. It was now a matter of purifying and closing the family's auric field so that the man could no longer intervene in an arbitrary and stressful way.

The intense accompaniment of suicides in this healing work can be a very stressful task because even the most loving efforts can be exhausting. This in turn opens the door for a new possession. But a vigilant and conscious approach to this problematic area protects the survivors and forms a healthy foundation from which real help can be offered to the deceased.

Summary

The burdens and possessions caused by the dead in the soul world can have different degrees of severity in the earthly world. They can affect places, landscapes, people, social groups, institutions and companies. On a personal level, they can make themselves felt both spiritually and physically. Just as with the etheric world, we are called upon to be attentive to ourselves and our environment. We are responsible for our own soul as well as for the surrounding soul world, and we can always have a healing effect on them. Moreover, we are never alone in our efforts. As will be shown in the following chapters, angelic beings, as well as many deceased people from the higher soul and spiritual worlds, are always at our side.

13

Time in the
Upper Soul World

I have looked into the deepest depths of man.
I know the world to its foundation stones.
Its meaning, I have learned, is Love alone
And I am here to love and ever love again.

Christian Morgenstern, 'We Have Found a Path'

Rudolf Steiner describes the journey through the soul world as a path of development through different planetary spheres. These are regions in the spiritual world that not only correspond to different levels of consciousness, but also to specific qualities, for example, morality, religiosity and spirituality. Depending on their development, the deceased can have intense, light-filled experiences of being in harmony with spiritual beings and other deceased persons, or suffer the most profound loneliness and isolation. They become aware of what their earthly life signifies for the whole spiritual world.

The length of time spent in the soul world varies from individual to individual and depends mainly on the level of development they have acquired during their incarnation.

Friends and relatives of the deceased sometimes assume that the duration of the stay in the soul spheres amounts to one-third the length of a person's earthly life, and then attempt to calculate precisely where they believe their loved one should be in their life review. However, Rudolf Steiner's statement of its duration is not a fixed formula but a relative average, which in no way excludes any deviations.

Attending to deceased persons in the soul world has shown me that this period can vary from one individual to the next by years, even decades. The inner maturity of the deceased and their ability to adapt to life in the soul and spirit worlds, make possible an ever more individual shaping of their development after death.

Not only are there human beings in the soul world who spend an unusually short or an exceptionally long time on their life review, but there are also souls who take on further tasks in the spiritual world in parallel to working on their last incarnation. These are spiritually mature souls who are deeply concerned with the world and who take an active, conscious part in its evolution. Many of these souls are able to work relatively quickly on their personal issues because already during their last incarnation they had honestly and consciously confronted their soul's shadow elements. Now they are able to devote themselves to other tasks, such as tending to those who have just crossed the threshold, particularly victims of natural catastrophes or accidents.

There was a man who died at the age of eighty-four. He had been dedicated to his work, was receptive to others and extraordinarily open to spiritual phenomena. After only two years, and in parallel with his life review, he began to dedicate himself to helping people who had lost their lives in catastrophic events: for example plane crashes or terrorist attacks. Together with other spiritual beings, this deceased person helps them overcome their shock and disorientation, and enlightens them about spiritual conditions.

Advanced souls in the soul world can also help certain human communities in their social activities. For example, they can support groups committed to the welfare of the earth, such as those concerned with environmental protection.

One woman who died in her mid-thirties dedicated herself to tasks related to healing the earth. She had crossed the threshold less than a year before. In her earthly life she had been an extremely sensitive, spiritually inclined woman who had worked intensively with the earth to harmonise life and landscape energies. After a very concentrated life review, she placed herself at the disposal of groups who worked in a similar way to heal the environment. Along with angels and elemental beings, she can work in the earth's aura to clean and heal the etheric atmosphere of polluted places.

Where specific developmental and healing processes are concerned, human beings in the soul world can help not only groups but also individuals, as the following example demonstrates.

A young doctor died at the age of thirty-three. He had been a spiritual seeker with a pronounced interest in anthroposophy and the art of healing. Following his death, he passed quickly through his life review, and after only three years he made himself available to help those deceased persons who had become trapped in the etheric and soul worlds. He also took part in healing processes when living doctors sought appropriate spiritual collaboration.

The range of tasks undertaken by such advanced souls are countless and freely chosen by them. The work they engage in corresponds to their nature, their spiritual interests, and the abilities they acquired during their last incarnation. Not only do they have a truly clear, strong impulse towards selfless work in certain areas, but also the necessary spiritual power. This power comes from their deep understanding of the world as well as from a sincere love for the good, the beautiful and the true, as encountered in the spirit of Christ.

Deceased people from the higher soul world appear as a concentrated focus of consciousness with hardly any form. They are diaphanous and light-filled, unencumbered by their personality traits. Nevertheless, they are easy to recognise as their nature always has something distinctive about it. They possess a much greater flexibility and react very quickly in communication. They can appear out of nowhere, act directly and efficiently, and just as quickly withdraw. They *want* to help. Their very willingness to be actively involved works like a surplus of power through which they can easily move back and forth between different tasks in different fields of consciousness. Therefore we can ask them for help in a particular task if we know that they are available. It is not necessary to have known them during their lifetime; it is possible to have the first encounter with such a deceased soul in the soul world during meditation.

In my experience, the help of advanced souls in the higher soul and spirit worlds is indispensable in the active spiritual work of people. The dead themselves experience it as a joyful fulfilment when we integrate them into a collective activity in which they can contribute their powerful and healing abilities. They can become our intimate spiritual friends, with whom we become active in a newly shared consciousness, promoting and helping the evolution of the world.

14

Leaving the Soul World

Whoever once free
from the great madness
gazes into the empty eye
of the Sphinx,
forgets the seriousness
of the earthly
out of supernatural
and just smiles.

Christian Morgenstern, 'The Knowing One'

The more a soul works to cleanse itself of its purely personal aspect, the more it progresses in the soul world. Figuratively speaking, the soul divests itself step by step of the soul garments in which it was clothed and which formed its inner life on earth. The more oriented it was towards the spiritual world in its earthly life, the more it is able to consciously shape this process.

The last stage in the soul world is a region which Rudolf Steiner calls the Sun Sphere: a world of sounds and spiritual harmonies in which the human soul has discarded most of what was closely related to it. The original Christian ideals of compassion and understanding for all creatures, openness of heart and tolerance towards all religions now form the basis of conscious perception. If on earth the soul has embraced the humanity of all people in the sense of seeing Christ in them, then it recognises here 'the meaning of all the interplay between the starry realms in the cosmic harmony and melody'.[5] The primordial laws of existence are revealed. The Sun Sphere prepares the human being to leave the soul world and to enter the spiritual world proper, which Rudolf Steiner sometimes calls Devachan.

Just as the human being had to discard their physical body when leaving the physical world, and their etheric body when leaving the etheric world, so now they are about to discard their soul body. Only a compressed essence, the quintessence of their soul, remains as the result of what they have worked on, and this will be available to them for later incarnations.

When leaving the soul world, deceased human beings expand further into the spiritual cosmos, becoming bigger and bigger until they span the entire realm of spiritual space. They have become the universe. At the same time, the whole cosmos turns itself inside out, so that the deceased now perceives it within themselves, within their vast nature. They look inwards, so to speak, at the earth and all the planets, at the entirety of cosmic space that is now within them. In Devachan, human beings form the outer world, whilst what was formerly around them on earth is now their inner world.

The transition from the soul world to the spirit world, to Devachan, is of a much greater and more overwhelming magnitude than the transition from the etheric to the soul world. Although it is true that the human being has already experienced an inversion of their inner and outer worlds in the soul world, here we are dealing with a more fundamental reversal: the core of the human being's own being now becomes a spiritual universe, and the universe itself in turn becomes their innermost being.

This is a process that can hardly be described. If we follow this process inwardly, we initially have the impression that our being is about to dissolve and evaporate and lose itself in the cosmos. In meditation, however, we can develop the strength needed to overcome this fear of self-loss and follow the path of expansion and inversion.

The human being has now become a spirit among spirits: In this sphere they experience the other human beings in Devachan expanding as they do. They interpenetrate one another and work together in developing and shaping our earth.

15

In the Heavenly Sphere

Do not stand at my grave and weep; I am not there.
I do not sleep. I am a thousand winds that blow.
I am the diamond glints on snow.
I am the sun on ripened grain. I am the gentle autumn rain.
When you wake in the morning's hush, I am the swift uplifting rush
Of quiet birds in circled flight.
I am the soft stars that shine at night.
Do not stand at my grave and cry; I am not there. I did not die.

Mary Elizabeth Frye

The word Devachan comes from Sanskrit and refers to the divine heavenly world. *Deva* means God and *chan* means an area, or dwelling. It is a world of majestic beauty that cannot adequately be described using our earthly concepts and images. It is a world of sounding tones, of the music of the spheres and their celestial harmonies. From here, the forces of the universe form a living, pulsating world rhythm, a harmonious unison that permeates and enlivens all existence. The highest hierarchies live and work here together with human beings in their life between death and rebirth.

In the soul world, the human being was predominantly

occupied with coming to terms with their own soul life. They came to understand that without exception our subjective experiences have objective consequences for the world. They acquired an understanding of themselves and their life as it was lived on earth that went beyond a purely personal perspective.

The consciousness they gained in this process now, in the sphere of Devachan, becomes an inner luminosity by which they can perceive the world of the spirit. Their ability to illuminate and recognise these spiritual realms therefore depends on the strength of their consciousness. Once again, how they stood within earthly life – their openness to spiritual matters, their connection with the being of Christ – determines their alertness in these realms.

In the soul world the deceased were focused mainly on themselves: what was within them became their outer environment. In the spirit world, they again experience themselves turned inside out: they are completely open and receptive to the world, which has now become their self. The feeling of being focused on themselves transforms here into a will-endowed, world-creating activity – providing they can sustain consciousness during this period.

The world of Devachan is a world of spiritual communities formed by many like-minded human beings as well as higher spiritual beings. Out of the expansiveness of their being, they concentrate their forces on a specific field of activity. Their aim is to prepare the earth's future. They are already on their way to a new life on earth, to a new incarnation, which will require certain earthly conditions. They are shaping the evolution of the earth, for their own sake and for the entire growth and development of humankind.

This shaping takes place, for example, through the human beings in that realm working through plant growth, through the elements, though light and natural phenomena. Rudolf Steiner describes this as follows:

> A plant nourished by the sunlight receives into itself
> not the physical light alone but in very truth the activity
> of spiritual beings, among whom there are also these
> human souls. These souls themselves ray down upon
> the plants as light, weaving as spiritual beings around
> the plants. Looking at the plants with the eye of the
> spirit, we can say: the plant rejoices at the influences
> coming from the Dead who are working and weaving
> around it in the light. When we observe how the
> vegetation on the face of the earth changes and ask how
> this comes about, the answer is: the souls of the Dead
> are working in the light which enfolds the earth; here is
> Devachan, in very truth.[6]

The deceased in Devachan also serve the earth in the cycle of the seasons, in the care of landscapes and in the design of places.

Twenty-five years after her death, a deceased person I had been close to, but with whom I had not kept in contact, appeared to me again quite unexpectedly. I sensed her presence, but could not 'see' her spiritually, as is usually the case with the dead in the etheric or the soul worlds. I concentrated all my heart power on her and noticed how I was expanding outwards with her, across the room and the house I was in, across the city and the landscape, across the earth and out into the cosmos. I was overcome with fear at first, but I managed to centre myself and let the events unfold. In this state of expansion, I experienced how the deceased spanned the entire world. At the same time, she was permeated by other beings who also existed in this expanded state. From there I could see the earth, surrounded by innumerable coloured, moving veils, which were formed by layers of diverse beings working together. The earth's landscapes radiated in the most varied forms and shapes. Whole 'nations' of spirit beings, large and small, worked with complete devotion on these formations, down to the finest detail. The earth shone like a great, breathing being. It was a living whole that consisted of the work and the light and the love of countless beings.

I turned to my companion and asked her what her role was in what was happening. As soon as I had asked this question inwardly, she pulled me down to earth in a flash. We found ourselves in a city unknown to me, in a small inner courtyard between two houses. It was a quiet, frosty night, and fresh snow lay on the ground. There she showed me how she 'swept' the snow, together with others from her group. They proceeded in such a way that they gently arranged the quietly falling snowflakes into a glittering white blanket that softly covered the earth. She also showed me how others in her group worked the air in this small courtyard so that it smelled of snow; the atmosphere became fresh and invigorating and the earth could breathe joyfully. Then I realised that in all our feelings towards the earthly world we experience the work of such deceased human beings in Devachan. What we perceive as a 'physical phenomenon of nature' is not only the work of elemental beings. When we see an enchanting snowy landscape, when we inhale an enlivening fresh breeze, we live entirely in the gifts and contact of these Devachanic beings. When we become aware of the beauty of our world, which is different day by day and that can make us deeply happy, we are directly experiencing the selfless actions of the dead in Devachan, their love for humanity and the earthly world.

Of course, the service of the deceased in Devachan is not limited to the earth. They are also active in the personal and social affairs of living human beings. They affect people's thoughts and feelings, they can inspire new ideas in art, therapy, medicine, pedagogy, science, politics, religion and so on. They can also inspire individual personalities, social initiatives, or social movements. Human beings are hardly aware of how concretely the spirit world works through them. The deceased are even happier when they can work hand in hand with individuals who are aware of their collaboration.

Not only in earthly realms are the deceased in Devachan active alongside other beings. They also involve themselves with other deceased souls in the afterlife and take on various tasks. They receive and help educate those who have just passed over the threshold and care for the souls of children who have died. They work in the various healing centres in the etheric and soul worlds in which the deceased in need of help reside, and they help redeem those who have become trapped.

Not all of the dead in Devachan have the strength to take part in this magnificent work. There are many souls for whom spiritual thoughts and feelings were something foreign during their life on earth. They did not develop an understanding of themselves as belonging to the entire world and of humanity as being grounded in the spiritual world. As a result, such individuals do not have sufficient strength to remain awake in the spirit world; they do not bring enough of their own light to consciously participate in all that takes place there. These dead in Devachan are therefore in an unconscious state: they 'sleep' through their time in heaven. Their angels hold and carry them and continue to work on their development, but the work that should be performed together, the angels do alone. These deceased are neither awake nor active in the Devachanic sphere.

On the other hand, people who have lived in earthly life out of their selfhood and have connected inwardly with the Christ impulse can work powerfully and consciously in the spiritual world. Their being can recognise and bear responsibility for the world's evolution, and they have the spiritual strength to serve the world in a supra-personal way. These shining and powerful humans form groups under the signs of great archangelic beings, and in accordance with the mission of each of these archangels, they move into the relevant areas of responsibility.

The deceased in Devachan who, for example, join the company of the archangel Raphael, work as healers as well as performing other tasks. The name 'Raphael' means 'God heals'. Raphael's work in the earthly realm is not only to heal and regenerate human beings on the physical, emotional, and spiritual level; he is also responsible for the processes of renewal and rejuvenation on the earth. Raphael's angels and the Raphaelite human beings who belong to him work accordingly.

The archangel Gabriel, who is the archangel of the Annunciation, is, among other things, the heavenly ruler over the powers of birth. Gabriel's angels and human co-workers accompany the souls of unborn children through pregnancy and birth. They also work in the powers of human hope, giving comfort and confidence.

One of the most powerful groups is the Michaelite dead. Michael means 'Who is like God?'. He is also called the 'Countenance of Christ'. He is the archangel of the sun and the representative of spiritual light. The human beings helping him work to bring humanity closer to Christ are involved in all processes that require courage and sacrifice. They do not only inspire the most diverse social, civic, and spiritual currents. Specific political peace efforts, organisations dedicated to the struggle for social justice and human dignity, associations committed to the protection of nature and the earth organism, and many more, are also stimulated by the Michaelites in Devachan. Moreover, they are the most potent helpers in the redemption of the dead and in the work against demonic and black magic forces.

These examples are mentioned in brief because all the archangels of light work towards the 'Christ-ening' of evolution on earth. They are joined by all advanced human souls in the soul world and in Devachan who make themselves available for the archangels' respective tasks. An exceedingly powerful Michaelite human being in Devachan described how this enormous world working is made possible out of a shared Christ consciousness:

> We form communities of light, united in the spirit as brothers and sisters of Christ. Our activity is an activity in Christ and with Christ, for he is the redeemer of the world. With him the entire development of the world takes place. From the highest realm of the Trinity he has descended into the deepest depths of the earth to lift the earthly world again to God the Father. We want to do this with him. With our entire being, we embrace the entire spiritual planetary system, knowing full well that there is a higher cosmic world: the world of the Father God, the principle of the Trinity. We feel this and want to serve him with devotion. Our service is the creation of the future. We move through developmental cycles that span immense periods of time with full awareness of the world as a whole. Through every act of will, we want to let the glory of heavenly creation infuse the earth. We are at one with the will of the world and live entirely in this gesture of love for the earth. It is our will to enlighten the earth, to love it, spiritualise it, illuminate it. Our identity consists of love for the world, selflessness and serving devotion.

Furthermore, this wonderful deceased person described the highest spheres of the Devachanic world. He himself, as part of a great spiritual community of monks, stimulates the spiritualisation of the earth:

> This world is the primal church of the world. The origin of everything religious is here. What you earthly human beings call spirituality originates here; everything spiritual refers to this realm of the truly spiritual. That which is called religion, meaning reconnection to the divine, has its origin in this sphere and carries within it the spiritual memory of what happens in this world that streams with light and wisdom. The World Temple is here. The highest hierarchies are turned in praise towards the Trinity, in a holy cosmic mass. Here the cosmic mass is celebrated. Humanity's masters and highest initiates live in this sphere and serve in God's heavenly Temple. From this place they direct earthly destinies, regardless of whether they are incarnated on earth or not. The source of everything is here; the earth is only a reflection.

But how can we incarnated human beings raise our consciousness to this indescribably sublime light-filled world of the living saints? How can we even perceive the dead in Devachan? Since the human beings in this region have discarded their separate, earthly personalities, we can no longer reach them through the ideas we had about them from their time on earth. They are therefore much more difficult for us to grasp than are the deceased in the etheric or soul worlds. What we have known as their unique and characteristic nature no longer clothes them. They no longer have the traits of their last incarnation but are truly spiritual beings with a completely different dynamic and vibration. We can, however, learn to sense them as a spiritual presence and to recognise them at the core of their being. Of course, heartfelt love for their being or an intimate relation to a specific subject area opens the way to them. Encounters with the dead in Devachan can be profoundly moving. But when it comes to a shared spiritual work, no sentimentality or melancholy resonates in the encounter. The meeting takes place on a cordial level beyond the personal, with the deceased appearing as a concentrated spiritual presence. Working with them happens very quickly: the mutual exchange serves the common cause and then they immediately withdraw again.

We do not have to have known in life the deceased in Devachan to be able to work with them. Through a common concern and a firm intention to achieve something in a specific area, we can get to know the deceased in Devachan as spiritual beings and begin working with them. The prerequisite is that we are willing to work in the same field. Human beings in Devachan always act together with others from their spiritual group. They have an all-embracing consciousness and comprise the totality of a complex of topics. It is enough to have one of them as a contact person, who then appears together with others who make themselves available for the corresponding task. Because they are pure spirit, they no longer experience the restrictions we know on earth; they do not tire of an activity as those with physical bodies do, since their very being is spiritual will-substance.

Neither angelic beings nor advanced deceased individuals who are in direct connection with humanity on earth ever interfere with a person's free will. They do not work against or beyond the person's will. They always act in a liberating, protecting, advising or inspiring way. This means that they cannot become active in many areas without the will of living people. Only when a human being on earth makes themselves available and expressly asks them for help can they spiritually and powerfully intervene.

The deceased in Devachan perceive incarnated humans as variously strong or weak lights that shine out from the earth into the cosmos. They do not see our physical figures but our spiritual auras, which shine in various colours and strengths. The more purified and capable of love people are, the more their light shines out towards the spirit world. The more spiritual and willing they are, the more they can attract and partner with those in Devachan who have died. Most of all, the incarnated person's conscious connection with the Christ impulse gives light and spiritual nourishment to those in the heavenly spheres. When asked what earthly humans can do for the beings of the spheres, another deceased Michaelite in Devachan, with whom I work on the redemption of the deceased, answered me:

> The Christ consciousness and Christ experience of
> living human beings are of the utmost importance and
> help for us. The conscious deceased in Devachan can
> always perceive Christ. We Michaelites are in Michael
> and therefore also in Christ. But the more an incarnated
> person develops a Christ consciousness, the more
> the deceased in Devachan develop a corresponding
> consciousness of self in the spiritual world and are not
> merely connected to everything. This is of immense
> importance to us.

We owe the revitalisation of our world and its ever-new impulses to these people of the Devachanic spheres, who are our spiritual brothers and sisters in the truest sense of the word. But so that they can give the earth a bright future, they depend on us to include them ever more consciously in the inner light of our presence. Hence the great arc of humanity stretches between them and us. Together we form the two ends of the bridge between earth and heaven. An I-endowed, Christened consciousness on both sides creates the substance that connects life and death with each other.

At the end of this time in the Devachanic world, there follows a last important stage in the continuing development of the human being. Rudolf Steiner calls this stage the World Midnight Hour. Beyond the spiritual planetary system, which encompasses the realms of the soul world and Devachan, the deceased expands once more, now all the way into the starry cosmos. It is an unfolding into infinity, in which we refuel from the forces of the starry worlds. This is the climax of the individual's conscious upward development on their path after death. Accordingly, few deceased people experience this region with an alert consciousness. It is the highest spiritual sphere to which a human being can rise: it is the world of the Father God. The World Midnight Hour is, therefore, the human being's homecoming to the throne of the Creator God.

Here ends the human being's journey through the spheres after death. This culmination is at the same time the prelude for the path back through various levels of consciousness towards a new incarnation. The work of the human being, which until then had been directed entirely towards the world, now becomes concentrated again on the core of their being, where they have an infinitude for their inner life.[7] From here on, human beings are no longer 'deceased', but are instead 'unborn'.

16

The Dark Spirit Worlds

The loss of good has received the name 'evil'.

Augustine, *City of God*, XI, 9

No evil dooms us hopelessly except the evil we love, and desire to continue in, and make no effort to escape from.

George Eliot, *Daniel Deronda*

Just as a person can consciously choose to do good, they can also choose to do evil. To want the good for the world does not mean to do it; and yet a life lived with the good in mind is qualitatively different than a life directed towards egotism and the ruthless acquisition of power. Evil is a choice. It comes from a variety of sources and manifests in a number of ways, and, as with everything that emanates from human beings, has powerful spiritual effects.

When a person's egotism and self-love take precedence over the concern for others, when their greed and striving for power leads them to treat others with contempt and use them to serve their own ends, when they ignore the moral instinct inherent in every human being, then they are close to evil. Such people can be stupid or intelligent, naive or thoughtful, knowing or ignorant. They lack empathy for all other creatures. They have become a world unto themselves, their actions are entirely egocentric and revolve only around themselves. Everything else has little value or validity for them.

Just as our deepest humanity is rooted in Christ, so the dehumanisation of human beings is rooted in beings that stand opposed to him. Hence the 'I' of such a person is not anchored in Christ, but in the dark hierarchies. As has been mentioned, the progressive spirits of the hierarchies and those connected to them respect the free will of living human beings. Those who serve the adversaries, on the other hand, show no such respect: unasked and uninvited, they try to assert their dominance over people through their doppelgängers or by possessing them directly.

On the one side there is Ahriman's realm, whose hardening forces seek to cut us off from the spiritual world and imprison us in matter, and on the other there is Lucifer's empire, with its opposing tendency towards dissolution and the wish to tear us away from the earth before the proper course of our development here has been completed. We all carry aspects of these powers within us and are in manifold interactions with them, and we can remain pervaded by these forces in the afterlife. They are a part of human evolution and therefore have a legitimate place in our cosmos: they challenge us and thereby promote the development of human consciousness.

But there is also the kingdom of Sorat, which has a very different origin. It is the embodiment of evil and all black magic activity originates here. By 'black magic' we are not referring to witchcraft and satanic rituals that take place in some dark chamber somewhere. The Soratic effect infiltrates our current world to a much greater extent than assumed. There are

BRIDGES BETWEEN LIFE AND DEATH

numerous people who choose evil under the guise of self-interest and power and who enter into a bond with the forces of Sorat. Totalitarian governments that torture and murder their citizens, as well as mafia and drug cartels and terrorist organisations, are all spiritually inspired and permeated by black magic forces.

Through their connection with Sorat, those who have given themselves up in service to his kingdom at first experience an increase in power and prestige. If a person has committed themselves to such a system, then after death they are fed by those same forces and continue to serve the same goals. The more consciously they operate, the more a Sorat-inspired individual (that is, a black magician) can maintain consciousness in Devachan. This consciousness, however, is not located in the light-filled spirit world, but in the corresponding counter-sphere of Sorat. Over time the person realises that their self-awareness has become hollowed out and they are tortured by this. What surrounds them is a world of darkness and spiritual beings of a demonic, destructive nature. Not knowing how to leave this sphere, they cling to it even more in despair. Unlike those human souls in the light-filled spheres of Devachan, who selflessly serve the earth and humanity, the Soratic dead try to maintain and expand their power systems for themselves. For this purpose they possess people with whom they have an inner resonance; they also infiltrate existing social structures and use them accordingly. But it is not only those systems that obviously violate the commandments of our humanity that are affected. The work of such counter-forces is also reflected in many phenomena of our time, for example in banking and economic structures, in tribal and nationalist politics, in the deification of greed and possessions, and in the decline of ethical-social values. It is also at work in some areas of modern technology.

Goethe's Faust sold his soul to the devil. The people who devote themselves to black magic have gone one step further: they have sold their innermost self, their *I*, to Sorat. But as with Faust, this is not the end of the story. The dark can always be redeemed by the light. It does not help to retreat in fear and wring our hands in anguish over the world. The only helpful thing here is to intervene with a clear, light-filled consciousness. The more we recognise the needs of this world and realise the good we can do when we ground ourselves in Christ, the more we learn to illuminate and redeem the dark corners of our world. The responsibility for our earth lies in our hands and we can make it our purpose to work with the light-filled souls in Devachan for the good of our world and its future.

17

How Do We Perceive the Dead?

However, the spiritual cannot be taught;
the spiritual must be implemented.

Viktor Frankl, *Der leidende Mensch*

Our early environment has an enormous influence on our basic attitudes towards life and death. Our parents' views and habits, the traditions of our family, what we experienced in our childhood and the customs of our native culture have laid the foundations of our attitude to these fundamental questions of human existence.

As a child, I sometimes dreamt about relatives dying. After waking, I would tell my mother about them. She would sit me on her lap and speak very naturally about the fact that, of course, people must go back to heaven. When another dream announced the death of my great-grandmother, my mother said to me: 'She is old and has grown tired of the earth; her soul wants to return with her angel to heaven. There she will become young again and gain new strength. You don't need to be sad about it.'

I was already sad when great-grandmother died three days

later, but I experienced neither dismay nor fear. The melancholy that sometimes crept in repeatedly gave way to trust in the rightness of this event and thus I learned to view death as a natural part of life. I understood, even if not yet consciously, that it was not a sudden break, but a process that has both a meaning and a goal.

Another scene, even earlier in my childhood, had a profound impact on me concerning death. My father came home one evening and said. 'Children, get dressed, we are going to church. Someone who has died is laid out. There is no one there, only the candles are burning, and the silence in the church is very special.' We went there and saw a man in his mid-sixties in a white shirt and grey suit lying in an open coffin on a table. His hands were folded on his chest; a fine, beautifully embroidered white cloth covered him up to his knuckles. His facial expression was quite peaceful. The whole atmosphere was calm and dignified. Candles were burning and at dusk the last rays of sunlight shone in through the coloured windows. My father held our hands firmly, and we looked at this stranger in silence for a long time. Since we did not know him, we did not feel any personal pain, but only deep amazement and reverence for the remarkable phenomenon of death. There was nothing frightening in any of this; a sustained holy silence lay over the event. I remember my father's warm hand holding mine the whole time, reassuring me, making me feel secure. Then my father whispered to us: 'How beautiful a human face is. Look, it is as if he is sleeping peacefully, isn't it? But there is only his body left. His soul is no longer here, it is on its way to heaven. And there are many angels here, even if we can't see them.' Listening to my father's words, I had the unmistakable feeling that they were true. I understood that this person's life had been completed and that death had opened a new door for him.

I am deeply grateful to my parents for these experiences, which laid the foundation for me to be able to deal with death in a respectful, positive and fearless way. Other children are not so fortunate in their upbringing. After the death of her grandmother, one of my nieces told me that her grandmother would visit her sometimes. The little girl was five years old and she told me in her thin little voice: 'You know, she's floating up on the ceiling in my room. And she says nice things to me. Granny is very, very sweet. She comes often, but everyone says: "That can't be, Grandma is dead."' I asked her what her mother had said about that. Looking very sad, the girl answered: 'Mama says I'm crazy.'

The impressions that we receive from those around us can therefore be quite different. Children often feel the approach of someone's death; they also often perceive those who have died, even if they cannot express this. We adults bear a responsibility for how we respond to them in these situations. We can be open to their experiences and help them grow in understanding, or we can be close-minded and cut them off from a profoundly important part of life.

It makes sense for us, too, to examine how our childhood and upbringing have shaped us in relation to death. Are there hidden experiences in our soul that we have not yet come to terms with? Is there some obstacle in us that we still need to overcome? To be able to deal with death in a healthy and harmonious way, we need an accepting attitude towards it. To be able to cope with illness and infirmity, loss and death, is necessary in developing a stable and emotionally mature approach. The belief that the deceased are with us and that they are close to us after their death enables us to approach the spiritual side of this event with our understanding.

It is also important to recognise and differentiate our feelings when it comes to any particular death. The pain of separation and loss is part of the experience of losing someone and is therefore entirely justified: we must give ourselves time to grieve and to heal. But we can also pay attention to why we are mourning. Are we grieving for the deceased person, for the fact that their life has ended? Or do we mourn for ourselves, for our loneliness and for our unfulfilled hopes and expectations? The more we are aware of our soul's emotions, the more we can recognise the quality of the pain. When I mourn over myself, I am trapped in my own soul life and do not perceive the reality of the spiritual world. If, however, I silence my soul for a few moments and earnestly think of the deceased, then it may become possible for me to sense completely different moods, which may even lift me out of my grief. Only then do I begin to feel the new world of the deceased.

After a death, it can be helpful to pay attention to which specific memories occur, which thoughts circle around us or which unexpected feelings become more noticeable. We can pay attention to the moods and subtleties of our everyday life, to conditions of light and scent, and to small events to which we would not otherwise have paid much attention: a bird singing on the windowsill, a blossom opening before our eyes, a soft breeze caressing our skin. All of these things do not happen by chance, but are hints of what is happening spiritually in and around us. It is not uncommon for deceased people to make themselves felt subtly through such events. Even if this should be unusual, we can follow our perceptions without over-interpreting them and deal with them attentively. They train our vigilance and teach us the language of inner silence.

The next possible step is to seek a deceased person consciously. This is possible through devotion and prayer, concentration and meditation. The first perceptions that we have about spiritual connections are barely perceptible. They often go unnoticed within the swift flow of our thoughts and feelings. We are used to directing our attention and sensory impressions outwards and we often dismiss as self-generated what comes from our own inner world. But beneath the surface of these everyday sensations, even if hidden at first, genuine impressions can also mingle.

The fear of our own inner life and of the spiritual world itself prevents us from establishing a concrete connection with these higher worlds. Doubts, a lack of self-confidence, or a denial of the spirit are products of the Ahrimanic parts of our doppelgänger. Thoughts like 'I can't do something like that,' or 'I've never had spiritual experiences before,' or quite simply 'I don't believe in it,' form a barrier to perception. Other people's questioning of inner experiences ('That is atavistic') and their judgements about it ('It's all in your head') originate from the same Ahrimanic forces of doubt and negation, often mixed in with envy and even a subliminal hatred for the spiritual abilities of others. Of course, we do not have to take at face value what others have said. A person without fears and prejudices nevertheless probes with interest and an open heart.

Another source of danger in dealing with spiritual experiences lies in the temptation to overestimate our perceptual capacities and to interpret our experiences in a way that is self-serving. This expresses the Luciferic aspects of our doppelgänger, whose task it is to fool us with illusions and lead us to false conclusions. Sound emotional health and a balanced mental and physical state are the foundation for reliable perceptions. A state of absentmindedness or inner disharmony, or a state of stress or strain, are not good conditions under which to conduct meditative work. Personal curiosity, subjective ideas and expectations, wishful thinking and the need for recognition also generate a great deal of self-involvement and leave no room for the spiritual that comes towards us. Last but not least, speculative explanations and contrived interpretations of what we have experienced complete an inept, unhealthy approach.

Many people may ask themselves whether their perceptions are right or wrong. The answer is simple: there are no wrong spiritual perceptions as such. Everything we perceive does exist as a soul-spiritual reality. What we need to be unstintingly thorough in determining however is: 'What did I perceive?' and 'Is this really what I think it is? Or is it perhaps something completely different, something self-generated?'

To be able to check ourselves here conscientiously, it is essential to follow a clear and careful approach in meditative work. With practice, this succeeds over time. Rudolf Steiner states: 'The capacity to determine what is "real" and what is "illusionary" in these higher regions comes only from experience, and such experience must become our own in a quiet, patient inner life.'[8] Since experience only comes through practice, people who, for fear of error, shrink from doing anything will not be able to establish a self-guided connection to the spiritual world. Without a fight, they surrender the field to the opposing forces, who justifiably regard this as a victory. Just as the little child cannot learn to walk without repeatedly falling, and just as we cannot learn to play a musical instrument without repeatedly failing, neither can we learn to train our spiritual organs of perception without clumsiness and missteps. There is no way to reach a state of perfection, so making mistakes is not the problem. Not realising this simple fact is.

18

Exercises

We should not think mystically about meditation, but then neither should we think of it lightly. It must be completely clear what meditation is in the modern sense. It also requires patience and inner energy of soul. Above all there is something else that belongs to meditation, something that no one can give to another human being: the ability to promise oneself something and then keep that promise. When we begin to meditate we begin to perform the only really fully free act in human life . . . In this we are completely free. Meditation is an essentially free act.[9]

Rudolf Steiner

There are diverse ways to practise perceiving the dead. In his books and lectures Rudolf Steiner describes three stages of higher spiritual consciousness: Imagination, Inspiration, and Intuition. These stages in higher knowledge have been discussed many times in anthroposophical literature, but implemented in practice only to a limited extent. They have not yet been widely established as a method of dealing with the deceased and with other spiritual beings. Furthermore, this path of higher knowledge is one that is suited to the particular soul constitution of modern humanity and the demands of contemporary life.

The level of Imagination refers to spiritual seeing: a beholding that enables the perception of true ideas and beings in the higher worlds. Even without external sensory perception, the human soul can shape impressions into internal images. In the Imaginative world, this involves perceiving an abundance of beings and events. The images appear to us

> in exactly the same way as if a sensory object were making an impression. They are as vivid and as true as sensory images, yet they are not of material, but of soul-spirit origin ... It is evident that individuals must first acquire this faculty of forming *meaningful images* without sense impressions. This is accomplished through meditation.[10]

The first step in working with the deceased is, therefore, to behold in a spiritual image the person who has crossed the threshold. As a meditative preparation for this, we must first create an inner space in which this encounter can take place. We can invite the deceased, together with their angel, into this spiritual space. How they appear to us, their size and form, the luminosity of their figure or the darkness that emanates from them, their mood and the nature of their surroundings, all of this give us information about their state and spiritual location. As an echo of these first impressions, we can immediately trace in our heart which feelings the deceased triggers in us. Do we have feelings of detachment, lightness, mobility and joy, or does our heart feel depressed, cramped and immobile? We can observe which beings surround the deceased. Their character and play of colours can also give us valuable information about their situation.

This spiritual picture of the deceased and their surroundings is indispensable for working with them; it cannot be replaced by theoretical assumptions or by personal ideas. As Steiner says:

> It is not possible to make real progress in penetrating higher realities without going through the stage of Imaginative knowledge ... This stage is unavoidable, because those who seek communication with the higher world without having passed through it can do so only unconsciously and are condemned to fumbling in the dark. We can acquire some faint sense of this higher world without Imagination ... but we cannot come in this way to true knowledge in full consciousness and bright, luminous clarity.[11]

Building on the first meditative step, the stage of Inspiration now follows. Steiner says of this: 'Just as Imagination may be called a spiritual *seeing*, so may Inspiration be called a spiritual "hearing".[12] No physical-acoustic process is meant here, but rather an inner understanding of the meaning of Imaginative experiences. The beings that are seen reveal their meaning and significance.

The spirit working behind the picture becomes perceptible and we begin to comprehend what we have so far perceived pictorially. The events are expressed in a language that we perceive as a realisation of thoughts within ourselves:

> If we were to compare what is now experienced with something in the physical world, we could come only close to explaining the matter by referring to something that does not exist at all in that world. Suppose it were possible to perceive the thoughts and feelings of another person without hearing any words with the

physical ear; such a perception might be comparable to a direct comprehension of the Imaginative element called 'hearing' in the spiritual sense. What 'speaks' are the colour and light impressions. In lighting up and dimming down, in the colour metamorphosis of images are revealed harmonies and discords that unveil the feelings, representations, and thought life of soul and spirit beings. Just as tone becomes speech in physical human beings when thought is imprinted on it, so do harmonies and discords of the spirit world grow into manifestations that are definite thought entities.[13]

In a direct encounter with a deceased person, this means that the nuances of their luminosity, the subdued or pure translucency of their figure, the impression of warmth or coldness that they create, correspond to their state of being. All this reveals itself *within* the person meditating through 'essential thoughts'. Hence a dialogue begins between the meditator and the deceased, which takes place in a kind of 'exchange of thoughts'. This is comparable to a conversation between two living people, except that it is not an externally audible communication, but an inner dialogue. To the questions directed to the deceased, the meditator receives answers in the form of thought-formations. The meditator begins to 'hear' what is going on inside things.

In life a good conversation only arises through loving attention to the other. It is shaped by questions, mutual exchange and above all by *listening*. The meditator proceeds likewise. We turn to the deceased with interest and active questioning. In this shared 'conversation' we can experience the situation in which they find themselves, what needs and concerns they have, whether they are in conscious connection with their angel or other beings. Our task is to listen in an intensive and receptive way, without interpreting or judging what is observed. The situation of the deceased is best revealed through close attention, an openness of heart and compassion.

However, this exchange does not take place one-sidedly. The meditator can also convey specific concerns to the deceased and, if needed, help clarify their situation. Redemptive work starts here. Beyond educational efforts, it involves giving active spiritual help to the deceased, such as involving other helpful beings, consciously connecting them to their guardian angel, dissolving 'possession' by other spiritual beings and accompanying the deceased into higher spheres. What is required of the meditator here is selflessness in perception, inner activity without self-interest and a trained sense of truth regarding their spiritual perceptions.

In regular work with the deceased in the etheric and soul worlds, these first two meditative steps of Imagination and Inspiration are sufficient. The deceased person who has crossed the threshold is still a soul being in these two worlds. For this, an Imaginative and Inspirational state of consciousness offers a sufficiently clear and well-founded basis to be able to assess the situation of the deceased, to come into a mutual exchange with them and, if necessary, assist them. The higher stage of Intuition *can* be used here as it enables an even deeper insight into the essence of the deceased, but in ordinary cases it is not needed.

Dealing with the deceased in Devachan, however, requires the ability to put ourselves in their place. This is only possible with the faculty of Intuition. The deceased in Devachan are no longer soul beings, but spiritual I-beings: pure spirits at one with the world and living directly in unity with other deceased in Devachan. Such a deceased spirit is not someone we meet opposite us or face to face, at least not as a rule, but instead lives in our environment. To grasp them, we must be able to place ourselves directly into their being, and this is only possible through Intuition.

Intuition is no longer about experiencing the characteristics and meanings of certain spiritual beings, but about connecting with them in such a way that we become one with them. We merge with another being and with their actions. We are no longer *outside* a specific context but *within* it. As Steiner explains: 'Thus, to enter all things, one must first step outside the self. We must become "selfless" in order to blend with the "self", or "I", of another being.'[14]

In meditation, this process takes place by leaving behind our own point of view of the deceased and entering into the position of the deceased themselves. In fact, this means that we consciously and deliberately slip *into* the deceased. Rudolf Steiner notes here: 'When it is said of Intuition that "through it we slip gradually into things", this is literally true.'[15] This procedure seems unusual at first. In some respects it is comparable to a role in a play which involves you putting yourself into another character's shoes. You immerse yourself in this other individuality and identify with it for a few moments. The decisive difference is that on the Intuitive level of perception it is not just a matter of thinking and feeling into another character. Here we do not play another role but become one with another being: we experience their essence in our own being.

Our self is not abandoned in this process, however. On the contrary, our self-awareness must be maintained: 'Any "loss of oneself" in another being is harmful. Therefore, only the "I", highly fortified within itself, can plunge into another being without damage.'[16] A healthy, prudent, stable inner life of our own is therefore of decisive importance for this meditative step. It is essential and indispensable for the sound health of meditative work to consciously return to our own being after such a change of position on the Intuitive level of perception and to deliberately anchor ourselves there.

It is to be noted that these three stages of Imagination, Inspiration, and Intuition correspond precisely to the human being's three steps in the afterlife. A deceased human being experiences their retrospective of life in the etheric world in Imaginations: the images of their life show themselves to the deceased in all their fullness and totality, presenting the characteristics of their earthly biography. In the soul world, the deceased comprehend the effects of their earthly life and its significance for the world through Inspiration. In Devachan the deceased becomes one with the world. They experience themselves in perfect harmony with other Devachanic beings and experience the entire world as their own being in an Intuitive way.

Rudolf Steiner points out that in meditation we trace the path of the human being's development after death:

> The same thing happens to a human being in meditation
> as happens in death. Only gradually can we recognise
> the enormity and power of what we undertake in
> meditation; can we recognise that we breach the deep,
> powerful mystery of death when we devote ourselves in
> the right way to meditation.[17]

From this we can see the importance of practising this meditative path when working with the deceased.

19
Methodology in Redemptive Work

Those who have remained behind on Earth have a far greater influence on the dead than the dead has on himself or others who have also died have upon him … It is really the individual who has remained on the physical plane, who had established some relationship with the dead, who through human will is able to bring about certain changes in the condition of souls between death and rebirth.[18]

Rudolf Steiner

The conscious connection of living people with those who have died is of great significance for both the living and the dead. The responsibility that we bear here is decisive, and our creative possibilities are manifold. When those left behind turn to the deceased with an open and loving heart, this can be a beneficial and healing experience for the deceased person. We can invite the deceased to participate in our spiritual thoughts and experiences. We can read spiritual texts to them or say prayers for them.

The deceased also enjoy the music or eurythmy we create for them, the paintings we paint, or the other artistic activities we perform for them. Deceased persons in need of help, that is souls who have remained trapped or are possessed, also need education and orientation regarding their further development in the afterlife. In more difficult cases, there is a need for active redemptive assistance on the part of living people.

Conventional literature dealing with possession by the deceased usually treats the inhabited living person as the victim and the deceased as the perpetrator. From a certain angle, this view is understandable, since the possessing soul, left behind in a world to which it no longer belongs, imposes itself upon the possessed. They deprive the living person of their etheric powers and force their own soul life upon them. Seen in this way, the inhabited person can indeed be viewed as the 'injured person'. But this perspective is one-dimensional. In reality, possessions are acts of helplessness, even if they are somewhat egotistical in nature, brought about in part by the deceased person being unable or unwilling to let go of their former life. Certain conditions relating to the living person also makes possession more likely to occur. The relevant criteria given below are few, but nevertheless decisive.

If there is a sympathetic resonance between the soul of the deceased and the soul of the living person, such as in the case of addiction, then possession may occur. The stronger the resonance, the more the living person attracts such a deceased soul. There is no need for a personal bond between the two; their unredeemed common issue is entirely sufficient as a cause. Here the possession points to a problem area on which the living person must work.

It can also happen that a living person has a severely weakened aura due to exhaustion or illness, which the deceased soul then penetrates and occupies. Here the task of the living is to develop an awareness of their auric sheaths, to strengthen them and to close them to foreign influences.

If relatives hold back the soul of the deceased, either through unprocessed grief or the inability to let go of the dead, then possession can also occur. The emotionally impure 'calling' of the deceased, as well as work within the family dynamic that has not been brought to a clean conclusion, can lead to the deceased remaining in the aura of the person concerned. Cases where relatives lovingly want to help a deceased person but are overburdened by this work, such as when tending a suicide, can also lead to possession. In such contexts, it is crucial to assess our soul powers correctly and create sufficient separation between ourselves and the dead.

Possession can cause a wide variety of emotional disorders in both adults and children, such as exhaustion, anxiety, panic attacks, depression, or abnormal behaviour, and they can also exacerbate illnesses and addictions. In social contexts, both within families and institutions, deceased souls can cause considerable interpersonal difficulties and act as an obstruction to social impulses. Last but not least, deceased people can occupy rooms, houses and places where we then feel uncomfortable and cannot develop freely. They can also disturb or block energies within the landscape, thereby burdening entire habitats of elemental beings.

Of course, not all such situations involve possession. In numerous cases, however, possession *may* be present, either as a cause or as a reinforcement. Each case should be examined individually and treated accordingly. To be aware that possessions exist and that they occur far more frequently than assumed is no reason to be afraid of dealing with the deceased. On the contrary, any possession can be dissolved, provided that the human being concerned is mentally healthy and willing to deal with it. It is important to realise that where possessions are concerned, most deceased are insecure and disoriented: they have missed a step in their development and, not knowing how they should progress, they remain stuck between worlds, quite lost. As soon as something appears that seems familiar or trustworthy to them, for example a place that gives them a sense of security or a person whose aura attracts them, this is a welcome opportunity for them to connect and find shelter there. Although angelic beings and deceased relatives surround them, they do not perceive them through the darkness enveloping their soul, and since their focus is still firmly fixed on the earthly world, they are much more easily drawn to living people with whom they can find some sort of sympathetic resonance. Therefore, we are the ones who are most able to help directly and to show these deceased souls their way into the spiritual world.

In this context, we cannot speak of deceased people being at fault as such. Instead, we need to show understanding and compassion for the situation of such needy souls. In addition, we are challenged to learn to perceive our environment – which includes both our surroundings *and* our own aura – and to nurture and purify it. In this way, redemption and healing can take place both for the deceased and for us.

There are many different approaches to dealing with the dead and with possession, from exorcism to lengthy, detailed post-mortem psychoanalysis; many other strategies lie between these two extremes. The aim of the exorcism of 'evil spirits' that the Catholic church has been practising for centuries has been to drive out demons from a person's aura. In many cases, however, it was a deceased soul who was trapped – no real distinctions were made. The exorcism violently removed the occupying spirit, but this did not solve the actual problem. The deceased person remained lost in the intermediate world close to the earth, with no one to help them find their way into the light. The knowledge that we can intervene in a spiritual event through our will, such as occurs during an exorcism, is valuable. But the violence of such action testifies to a fear in dealing with the world after death and ignorance about prevailing spiritual conditions.

The counterexample to this is a psychoanalytical treatment of the deceased who has become trapped. This approach was developed in the last century, first through mediums and hypnosis, later through clairvoyant therapists. What was new about this work was the recognition that the possessing spirits were usually human beings, hindered in their free will and in need of help, who needed to be treated with understanding as well as caution. The measures carried out in this instance resembled conventional psychoanalysis: the soul eventually recognises its problems and to the extent that it can accept them is able to draw close to the light. Whilst this methodology was well meant and is still practised today, we do not bring the soul forward in a meaningful way by repeated conversations and dwelling too long on unfree emotions. In addition, the living helper loses much time and strength, which they could have available for entirely different tasks.

Between these two extreme approaches of dealing with possession there lies a middle way. It involves establishing a healthy balance between a compassionate understanding of the problem and a clear-willed course of action guided by our fully conscious 'I'.

The approach within redemptive work is determined by three scenarios usually found in dealing with occupying deceased persons.

The deceased does not know how to proceed

In the first scenario, the deceased is unintentionally trapped. They are usually willing to leave the intermediate world in which they find themselves, but lack either orientation and clarity or the determination and courage to do so. With this category of deceased, the work of redemption proceeds quite easily and quickly. Listening attentively to their concerns and enlightening them about their situation is enough to lead them to the light. If, for example, such a soul is not yet aware that they have crossed the threshold, this should be made clear to them. If a specific matter or need holds them back, they should be told that to solve their problem they must step out of their current state. If they believe that they cannot or must not free themselves from their present circumstances, we can make it clear to them that they can leave the sphere in which they find themselves at any time. In this regard, they must make an intentional decision and accept the help offered to them by the spiritual helpers. Drawing the deceased's attention to their angel and to their deceased relatives who surround them is an effective way of achieving this. It is also useful to summon other beings who are responsible for such transitional situations and who accompany the deceased into the next sphere.

The deceased refuses to go any further

In the second scenario, we encounter dead people who are trapped or possessing others and who refuse to leave. They are strongly entangled in specific earthly connections and do not want to let them go. Here it is also important to listen to them and to understand their concerns, and then to enlighten them about their condition and its consequences. As has been described in earlier chapters, this can be done through the transmission of spiritual knowledge via the heart in a single impulse of the will. The transmission of knowledge in this way means that a deceased person can absorb virtually an entire encyclopedia of new thoughts, insights and emotions in just a few moments. Images flow into their world of perception that nourish them and help to bring them out of their confused state. It is then much easier to draw their attention to their angel or to other deceased souls whom they can now recognise.

However, there are situations in which, despite the assistance provided so far, the deceased still refuses to leave. Here the will of the living person must actively intervene and change the existing situation: the deceased must be forced to leave. We must bear in mind here that whereas the will of a living person is free, the will of a deceased person, who has remained entangled in earthly conditions, is not. They are imprisoned in their thoughts and desires. If such a deceased person burdens or harms people or places, they must be removed from them. This happens with the help of angelic beings and the deceased in Devachan who can be called in and who make themselves available for the work of redemption. Such spiritual beings connect with the free will of meditating human beings and work with their intention. They surround the deceased and lead them out of the area into which they have settled. We should follow the events and make sure that the deceased actually takes the step into a higher sphere accompanied by higher beings. If we merely send them away, they may leave the occupied place or the person to whom they are attached but continue to wander between the worlds without finding salvation. In this work we bear responsibility for not only dissolving the possession but also for freeing the occupying soul from their predicament.

The deceased and black magic

The third scenario in connection with redemptive work concerns the handling of black magic forces. This area requires a special approach. Beings that have permeated themselves with Soratic powers can be recognised by the fact that we immediately experience a very constricting, dark and oppressive effect in our heart and solar plexus. It feels as if our auric heart is suffocating. In the encounter with such beings, we see that they do not respect the sacred and they react to everything spiritual with ridicule and contempt.

I have had the awe-inspiring experience that when I speak the Lord's Prayer from the depths of my heart, all beings present, up to the Luciferic and Ahrimanic spirits, get down on their knees. Conrad Ferdinand Meyer has quite rightly captured this spiritual reality in his poem 'Ja' (Yes):

As through his new creation, the Lord swung
With a mighty swinging wing,
Spirits followed his flaming trail
In crowded rings.

His most beautiful angels greeted him
Heads bowed in silent bliss,
Giant figures of the night
Closed the circle below.

'Before I release your circle dance,'
The Omnipotent now spoke,
'Swear, good ones, swear, evil ones,
Only to do my will!'

The shining ones cheered joyfully:
'To serve you, we are there!'
Those who ruin, those who destroy,
The demons snarled, 'Yes.'[19]

Both the light and the dark hierarchies are creatures of the Father world, and it is truly the case that they recognise the Father God as the Creator of all existence. Though they are bound in different spheres of action, all beings know themselves united in a complete hierarchy whose order they respect. Soratic beings are the only exception. Sorat comes from another cosmos and, accordingly, those who have connected themselves with him view the guiding spiritual principles of our world as ineffective and irrelevant.

All creatures bow before the sign of the cross as the sacred symbol of Christ; but not the spirits that are permeated with black magic. They do not know the language of Christian love. They know neither reverence nor compassion. They cannot be welcomed with warmth of heart or disarmed with a stream of love like other dark beings. The only thing that renders them powerless is when we confront them with all the dignity and radiance of our own 'I'. Here they experience the untouchable essence of the higher 'I' and the powerful effect of human freedom. In the encounter with such beings we cannot, figuratively speaking, hide behind Christ Being. It is not enough to know that Christ is at our side; in a certain sense, we must let the Christ be raised up within ourselves. The following meditation can be an example of this way:

Christ who shines in my thinking,
Christ who lives in my feeling,
Christ who works in my willing:
Shine on me from head to heart,

Weave in me from heart to limbs,
Stream from limbs into the world,
That I behold your light-filled, loving nature,
Learn to live in your sacrificial will,
How it weaves working in human development.
And so I feel myself as a member of your being,
And permeated entirely by your stream of love:
Not my I – Christ wants to enter me![20]

It is possible to connect so profoundly with the essence of Christ that our entire spirit is permeated by it. This conscious power of the 'I' gives the power of uprightness and the necessary protection needed here. In this way, our 'I' becomes effective in its purest sense. From our centre, we are empowered to place *ourselves* in confrontation with the forces of Sorat and to actively withstand this encounter.

In dealing with people burdened by black magic, some important points must be considered. Our motive for carrying out redemptive work must be pure and objective: personal interests or a need for recognition must be absent as these furnish easy points of attack. Our mental condition must be calm and completely free of fear, instilled with a firm inner poise that can withstand the assault of Soratic forces. Beyond that, since hardly any human being is emotionally 'clean' and without weakness, spiritual protection is necessary. As has been mentioned, this is achieved through actively connecting our selfhood with the sustaining power of Christ. And last but not least, the deceased in Devachan should always be called upon for help as they have been prepared for a confrontation with black magic forces. They are the ones who carry out the actual redemption and purification work, but they need our will impulse for this.

Concluding redemptive work

The three categories summarised here roughly encompass the degrees of severity we encounter when dealing with possessing and trapped souls. Meditation in pairs or small groups can be helpful for this work: shared practice complements individual perception, the mutual exchange of experiences reflects the many-sidedness of what is perceived, and we learn to check ourselves more attentively. In this way, we can more easily see through and avoid one-sidedness and mistakes. Furthermore, the effect of meditative activity gains strength by a shared focus and effort of will.

What we should not forget in any meditative work – and therefore in any redemptive work – is to carry things to a clear and clean conclusion. This means offering sincere gratitude to all beings involved, even to the seemingly difficult ones. The deceased who are to be redeemed, the angels and the other helping beings all contribute to a process that has incredible value and meaning for each participant. The meditator's angel has carried them through the entire effort, so the angel too should be sincerely thanked. At the same time, we should be aware that every spiritual activity unfolds through the grace of a heavenly world that accompanies, illuminates and loves us always.

I always finish meditative redemptive work with a prayer, for example with the Lord's Prayer or with a Christ prayer, which I say together with the beings who are present. It is then a matter of consciously saying farewell to all those involved in the process and releasing them from our auric field. Just as we say goodbye to neighbours and friends after a visit and send them away from our home, so too our spiritual environment – our own aura within which this work has taken place – should become free again and remain closed until further notice. This procedure is an indispensable prerequisite for healthy spiritual work.

Conclusion

The things we see ... are the things which are already in us.
There is no reality beyond what we have inside us. That is why
most people live such unreal lives; they take pictures outside
themselves for the real ones and fail to express their own world.
One can of course live contentedly enough in that situation.
But once you know about the other, you no longer have the choice
of following the majority way. The way of the majority ...
is easy, ours is hard.

Hermann Hesse, *Demian*

The culture in which we live has a decisive influence on our understanding of the world and of ourselves. The current materialistic-scientific world view has created an image of human life as beginning at birth (or just before it at conception) and ending at death, thereby enclosing us entirely within earthly existence. This paradigm has defined human consciousness as the product of solely material processes and the limits of physical existence as impassable barriers, but the experiences of countless people contradict these claims. Spiritual experiences are increasing. It is no longer exceptional to hear of people who have memories from earlier incarnations, who have encounters with angels, elemental beings and even with Christ, relatives who experience their loved one beyond the threshold, women experience the nature of their unborn child.

When I give lectures or seminars about relating to those who have died, I often ask at the beginning of the event whether someone from the audience has already had experiences with the dead. As a rule, about half of the participants report their experiences. Some of them have only fleeting experiences, others more frequently; some have positive experiences, others have had more stressful ones. This indicates that perceiving those who have died is a real part of our lives. Many people experience the soul-spiritual threads that connect our worlds, but how often do such spiritual impressions flit past us? How often are the dead close to us and we do not even notice them?

Our five-year-old son, who, like many other children, has spiritual perceptions from time to time, asked me one day, 'Mama, what's the name of your dear old friend who went to heaven last year?'

'Do you mean Stephen?'

'Yes, Stephen.'

'What about him?'

'He's sitting on the roof of our house looking down at us. Don't you see him?'

I immersed myself into the spiritual environment and perceived my deceased friend. Of course, he was not 'sitting' on the roof of the house, but at that moment he shone as a great spirit figure over us and enveloped us with a warm, loving light.

A few months later, again in a casual conversation about his day in kindergarten, he said, 'It was good. We kept building the big sandcastle that we had started yesterday. By the way, Mama, Stephen passed by here yesterday afternoon. Didn't you see him?'

'No, I didn't see him yesterday. When was he there?'

'When you were vacuuming.'

'Aha. And what did he do?'

'He tapped you on the forehead for a moment. And you had a nice thought.'

How often do we receive unnoticed visits from the spiritual world? How often are we surrounded by our loved ones from beyond the threshold? How often do they caress us with a ray of love and give us their warmth? The deceased seek connection with us. They accompany us and give us gifts; they empower, inspire, and motivate us. They illuminate and help to shape our earth. But they also need our keen attention and our trusting friendship. Through us, they seek to be involved in the evolution of the world, and together with them, we are the creators not only of what our earth is but of what it will be.

Of course, there are also deceased souls who are sorrowful and depressed and who need our help and inspiration. The world groans under the weight of their inner darkness and reflects its suffering in the shadows of so many things happening on earth. But these deceased are also our human brothers and sisters; if we help them, they too can do more for the world.

We are connected to the world of the dead in an extraordinary way because together we form a *hierarchy* that reaches up through various levels of being and consciousness. Not only are we connected as living human beings on the level of earthly existence, we are also the link to all prenatal and post-mortal spheres. The human being, therefore, is part of a horizontal as well as a vertical social context and forms the cross of the world between heaven and earth. Our hearts are the intersection of this cross and our meeting place with others, and it is love that enables us to form a connection between people. To be aware of this spiritual connection and to meet it responsibly already builds bridges between the worlds.

Knowledge does not merely reflect existing reality, but also involves the human spirit's creative activity. Accordingly, contact with the world of the deceased that is perceptive and actively constructive, receptive as well as redeeming, creates bridges for the benefit of the entire world. The poet Manfred Kyber has captured this connection precisely in a most beautiful way in his poem 'The Dead':

> Build bridges in you to the land of the dead
> The dead build with you, constructing the earth
> Walk hand in hand with the dead, aware,
> So that the whole world will be filled with spirit.[21]

May we succeed in building this bridge!

The deceased did not die. Their vesture died.
Their bodies crumbled; their spirit and will live.
They are always united with you
In your soul's deep temple silence.

In you and in them rests a united realm
Where death and life exchange words.
In it, you can, like your own thinking,
Listen to the quiet voices of your dead.

And you can speak, as you once did,
Your words silently to your dead.
Our spirit's path is unchangeable
And the gate of death is eternally open.

Build bridges in you to the land of the dead
The dead build with you constructing the earth
Walk hand in hand with the dead, aware,
So that the whole world will be filled with spirit.

Manfred Kyber, 'The Dead'

Notes

1. www.who.int/mental_health/prevention/suicide/ suicideprevent/en
2. Rübeneck, Stefan P., 'Causes of Suicide'. In Federal Statistical Office Wiesbaden, in *Wirtschaft und Statistik*, 10/2007.
3. Steiner, *The Effects of Esoteric Development*, lecture of March 27, 1913, p.166.
4. Steiner, *From Jesus to Christ*, lecture of Oct 14, 1911, p.176f.
5. Steiner, *At Home in the Universe*, lecture of Nov 17, 1923, p.75.
6. Steiner, *The Theosophy of the Rosicrucians*, lecture of May 28, 1907, p.45.
7. Steiner, *The Inner Nature of Man*, lecture of April 13, 1914, p.135.
8. Steiner, *The Stages of Higher Knowledge*, p.5.
9. Steiner, *The Mystery of the Trinity*, lecture of Aug 20, 1922, p.80ff.
10. Steiner, *The Stages of Higher Knowledge*, p.4f.
11. Steiner, *The Stages of Higher Knowledge*, pp.18, 20.
12. Steiner, *The Stages of Higher Knowledge*, p.43.
13. Steiner, *The Stages of Higher Knowledge*, p.46f.
14. Steiner, *The Stages of Higher Knowledge*, p.8.
15. Steiner, *The Stages of Higher Knowledge*, p.7.
16. Steiner, *The Stages of Higher Knowledge*, p.51.
17. Steiner, *From the Esoteric School, Esoteric Lessons: 1910–1912*, p.166.
18. Steiner, *Between Death and Rebirth*, lecture of Dec 3, 1912, p.56.
19. Meyer, 'Ja' in *Ausgewählte Werke*, p.86.
20. Poeppig, 'Christus-Meditation' in *Yoga oder Meditation*, p.197.
21. Kyber, 'Die Toten' in *Genius Astri*, S. 41.

Bibliography

Frankl, Viktor, *Der leidende Mensch* [The suffering man] Huber, Bern 1984.

Goethe, Johann Wolfgang von, *Wilhelm Meister's Apprenticeship Years.*

Grillparzer, Franz, *Gedichte und Dramen* [Poems and dramas]. Elibron Classics, 2000.

Hesse, Hermann, *Demian*, (tr W J Strachan), Peter Owen; Vision Press, London 1958.

Kyber, Manfred, *Genius Astri. 34 Dichtungen*, Drei Eichen, Hammelburg 2001 (English: *Genius Astri*, (tr Rosamund Reinhardt), Vineyard Press, USA 1977.)

—, *Complete Poems*. Aurinia, Hamburg 2009.

Meyer, Conrad Ferdinand, *Ausgewählte Werke*, ed. Hermann Engelhard, Fackelverlag, Stuttgart 1988.

Morgenstern, Christian, *Werke und Briefe*. Vol. 1 & 2, Lyrik, (tr R H Bruce), Urachhaus, Stuttgart 2013.

Poeppig, Fred, *Stufen auf dem Wege. Aphorismen und Tagebuchblätter*, [Steps on the way. Aphorisms and diary pages] Bettina Woiczig, Vienna, 1963.

Poeppig, Fred, *Wege zu einem meditativen Leben. Sprüche, Gebete und meditative Texte*, [Ways to a meditative life. Sayings, prayers and meditations] Verlag Die Kommenden, Freiburg i. Br.: 1968.

Poeppig, Fred, *Yoga oder Meditation. Der Weg des Abendlandes*, [Yoga or meditation: the way of the west] Verlag Die Kommenden, Freiburg 1965.

Saint-Exupéry, Antoine de, *The Little Prince*, (tr Katherine Woods); William Heinemann, London, 1945.

Steiner, Rudolf, *At Home in the Universe: Exploring Our Supersenory Nature* (CW231), Anthroposophic Press, USA 2000.

—, *Between Death and Rebirth* (CW141), Rudolf Steiner Press, UK 1975.

—, *The Effects of Esoteric Development* (CW145), Anthroposophic Press, USA 1997.

—, *An Esoteric Cosmology: Evolution, Christ and Modern Spirituality* (CW94), SteinerBooks, USA 2008.

—, *From Jesus to Christ* (CW131), Rudolf Steiner Press, UK 1973.

—, *From the Esoteric School, Esoteric Lessons: 1904–1909* (CW266/1), SteinerBooks, USA 2007.

—, *From the Esoteric School, Esoteric Lessons: 1910–1912* (CW266/2), SteinerBooks, USA 2013.

—, *From the Esoteric School, Esoteric Lessons: 1913–1923* (CW266/3), SteinerBooks, USA 2011.

—, *Geist und Stoff, Leben und Tod* [Spirit and matter, life and death] (GA66), Steiner Verlag, Dornach 1989.

—, *The Inner Nature of Man and Our Life Between Death and Rebirth* (CW153), Rudolf Steiner Press, UK 2013.

—, *The Manifestations of Karma* (CW120), Rudolf Steiner Press, UK 2011.

—, *The Mystery of the Trinity* (CW214), SteinerBooks, USA 2016.

—, *The Stages of Higher Knowledge* (CW12), SteinerBooks, USA 2009.

—, *Theosophy of the Rosicrucians* (CW99), Rudolf Steiner Press, UK 1981.

—, *Truth-Wrought-Words*, Anthroposophic Press, USA 1979.

Before Birth and Beyond Death
The Transformation of the Human Being

Karl König

Karl König, following Rudolf Steiner's teachings, believed
that human beings are eternal and that our time in our earthly
bodies is just one part of our journey. Our souls exist before
birth and continue on beyond death until they are reborn.

In these important lectures and essays, König argues that the
greatest part of our community exists beyond this earthly
life. He calls on us not to neglect our connection with them
and encourages us to solicit their guidance so that we might
rediscover the values that our society has lost.

König suggests that by changing our everyday thinking, we can
create a bridge across the threshold of death, allowing essential
communication between humans in different states of being
and uniting humankind to the benefit of all.

florisbooks.co.uk

Approaching Death
A Companion's Guide to the End of Life

Renée Zeylmans

Just as no person is the same as another, each death is individual. This special book does not promote methodologies or theories, but rather offers insights, information and contemplations on the end of life. It supports the companions of those on their dying journey, whether volunteers, medical professionals, pastors or loved ones.

Renée Zeylmans taught courses on accompanying dying and bereavement for many years. She described the journey towards death as a reciprocal process, asking not only how do we travel with those who are dying and what can we give them, but what do they give us? This book is the fruit of a lifetime's work, and her intention was for it to enrich the reader, throw a new light on difficult situations, evoke recognition, console and offer choices.

florisbooks.co.uk

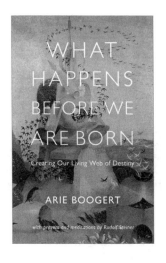

WHAT
HAPPENS
BEFORE WE
ARE BORN

Creating Our Living Web of Destiny

ARIE BOOGERT

with prayers and meditations by Rudolf Steiner

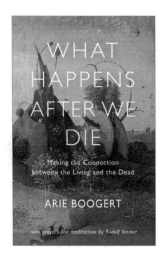

WHAT
HAPPENS
AFTER WE
DIE

Making the Connection
between the Living and the Dead

ARIE BOOGERT

with prayers and meditations by Rudolf Steiner

THE
NEAR-DEATH
EXPERIENCE

In the light of scientific research
and Rudolf Steiner's Spiritual Science

CALVERT ROSZELL
Foreword by George G. Ritchie, Jr.

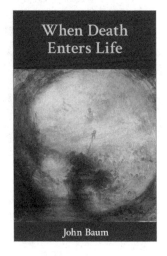

When Death
Enters Life

John Baum

Floris Books

For news on all our **latest books**,
and to receive **exclusive discounts**,
join our mailing list at:

florisbooks.co.uk/signup

Plus subscribers get a FREE book
with every online order!